The Research Revolution

The Research Revolution

LEONARD S. SILK

with an introduction by
WASSILY W. LEONTIEF
Henry Lee Professor of Economics, Harvard University

Illustrated by John Groth

McGRAW-HILL BOOK COMPANY, INC.
New York   Toronto   London   1960

THE RESEARCH REVOLUTION

"... The laws of science have
Never explained why novelty always
Arrives to enrich (though the wrong question
Initiates nothing) ..."

W. H. Auden

TO BERNICE, without whom...

Acknowledgments

Immediately, this book grew out of my special report *The U.S. Invents a New Way to Grow*, published in the January 23, 1960, issue of *Business Week*. But it really developed over a much longer period of time out of many articles and many arguments I had with my colleagues on the magazine. I am particularly indebted to Theodore B. Merrill, Jr., our industrial-production editor, for his brilliant special report *Semiconductors* of March 26, 1960, which backed up my piece on economic growth and convinced me that I had wrought better than I wot at the time; slightly rewritten, Merrill's report appears here as Chapter 4. I am also indebted to Dexter Keezer, Douglas Greenwald, and Robert Ulin of the McGraw-Hill Department of Economics (Ulin has since moved to the Socony Mobil Oil Co.) for their study *The Outlook for Expenditures on Research and Development during the Next Decade*, presented at the December, 1959, meetings of the American Economic Association; it appears

ix

here as the Appendix. For many insights into the working of our economy, for much good counsel, and for sympathetic but pretty merciless criticism, I wish to thank my colleagues, Elliott V. Bell, Kenneth Kramer, John L. Cobbs, Howard Whidden, Peter French, Clark R. Pace, Jane H. Cutaia, Robert B. Colborn, Lawrence H. Odell, Eugene Miller, Richard A. Wolters—but I had better arbitrarily stop there, though I am sure that many others will find something they once told me embedded here. Of course, these worthy gents should not be held responsible for anything that's wrong with this book; that's entirely my own fault.

I am grateful to Random House for permission to quote from W. H. Auden's *The Age of Anxiety*, which they published in 1946.

Leonard S. Silk

Contents

Introduction

For the generation that felt and still vividly remembers the full impact of the great collapse of 1931, the economic problem was how to avoid depression; today, however, it is how to achieve a satisfactory rate of growth. After the last war the high rate of growth was adopted as a long-run policy objective by so-called underdeveloped countries; now it has become a matter of serious concern to fully industrialized Western nations as well. Indeed, how could one disagree with the author of this book when he observes that "... too slow a United States growth would mean that the Soviet Union might succeed in its bid to achieve world domination through its own economic power"? How can one avoid being concerned with the economic development of the United States when even the sedate National Bureau of Economic Research finds that the present rate of growth of the Soviet Union is now the double of ours?

Some experts—or should one call them wishful thinkers?

—predict that our ambitious competitors must soon run short of breath and reduce their pace. There are also those who feel that, in order to keep the lead, we would have to give up the amenities and possibly even the freedom of our amateur status and turn professionals—that is, planners—which, they say, would be too high a price to pay to win an economic race.

In this book Mr. Silk, an experienced observer and interpreter of the contemporary economic scene, gives us hope. He describes the new force which enables our economic engine to step up its speed without undue strain. That accelerating factor is incessant technological innovation through scientific advance. The fastest growing American industry is large-scale research and the most rapidly expanding markets—the markets for new products, new materials, new know-how.

Mr. Silk's exciting story also shows that dependence on a perpetual flow of purposeful innovation creates new problems for business, for government, and for the American society as a whole. More problems will arise as the research revolution gradually permeates all aspects of our economic life. To one, possibly the most important, of these yet unanswered questions I dedicate these introductory remarks.

If continuous prosperity and healthy growth of the American economy, from now on, must increasingly depend on investment in scientific and technological research, how can we be sure, or make sure, that this particular kind of investment will expand sufficiently fast and that its results be actually put to best possible use? As the reader of this book will learn, venturous business—big, medium, and small—today earns a fabulously high average rate of return on the dollars it spends on research. This indicates, of course, that up to now the flow of funds into this kind of investment despite its rapid rise has not been sufficiently large. The story of semiconductors described in Chapter 4 and Dexter Keezer's statistics in the Appendix show that the rush is on; this means that, before long, the profitability gap between this and other kinds of productive investment will first diminish and then tend to disappear. From then on, sound business principles will demand that each additional dollar invested in research should earn not more and not less than additional dollars spent on acquisition of new machinery or, say, devoted to promotion of larger sales. The forces of healthy competition, if nothing else, will see to it that in an expanding economy new capital is allocated among the alternative investment opportunities in such amounts as to equate the average per dollar rate of return in all of them.

Will this—at least in the long run—result in a sufficient expenditure for research? For any other kind of productive investment the answer would be yes, but in this special case of investment in research the answer is unfortunately no.

So far as the general conditions of production are concerned, organized research is not different from any other industry. One builds a laboratory, installs the necessary equipment, hires qualified personnel, and waits for the results. These, like any other product, either can be used directly by the same business in which they were made or can be sold to others—for a price; or, as it often happens, both. In one respect, however, the product of industrial research, which is new scientific knowledge or technical know-how, differs from most other goods: It can be useful, it might turn out to be useless, but it cannot be used up. Not only can the same person make use of an idea, of some specific piece of technical information, over and over again without the slightest danger of exhausting it through wear, but the same idea can serve many users simultaneously, and as the number of customers increases, no one need be getting less of it because the others are getting more.

This unlimited, universal availability of knowledge and ideas produced by research is certainly a very desirable property for the society, for mankind as a whole. But it creates a serious problem for anyone who would like to engage in research, i.e., in the production of knowledge as a business enterprise. To justify investment in research a corporation must be able to sell its results directly—or indirectly, as a component part of some other product, for a price. But who would pay for a good which, once it has been produced, becomes available to everyone in an unlimited amount? Why not wait until someone else pays for it or invests in its production and then have a free ride?

The patent, the copyright, and the licensing laws take care of this. They provide the quantity dimensions for objects which intrinsically have none and thus make it possible for private enterprise to engage in the production of ideas and new knowledge and sell or use them profitably as one can use or sell steel or bread. This is an ingenious and, so far as it goes, a very effective solution of the problem; unfortunately, it is not quite effective enough. Under the patent and license system, the range of practical applications of new ideas is necessarily narrower than it otherwise could have been, and the total volume of human and material resources devoted to production of useful knowledge is necessarily smaller than it should be.

This becomes clear as soon as we ask what would happen if the producer of a new technical idea, after having, through the sale of licenses, recovered his expenses plus reasonable return on capital investment, proceeded to issue additional licenses at a reduced price. Potential customers who before could not afford to buy the new idea would now, of course, acquire it and put it to good use. Since reselling the same item over and over does not increase the costs of making it, all the additional receipts of the producer of the new idea will moreover be added to his net return on the invested capital. Not only would there be gain all around at once, but in the long run the higher rate of profit would most likely increase the total amount of capital invested in research.

What is described above is, of course, nothing else but price discrimination—a device often used to secure the largest possible market for a good or service, additional demand for which can be satisfied at ever smaller and smaller additional cost to the producer. Electric utilities practice it by lowering the price to large consumers, and railroads practice it by charging, not a flat ton-mile rate, but rather what the particular kind of traffic is able to bear. In utilization of ideas, additional demand can be satisfied by the producer at no additional costs at all. Some commercial research organizations, in fact, do tend to adjust their fees to the licensees' capacity to pay. When practiced by businesses which are not officially considered to be public utilities, differential pricing, however, is not strictly legal. But even if it were, in the case of such an unstandardized product as new technological ideas, a systematic attempt to discriminate between various uses would at once get entangled in mountains of red tape. Still this does not mitigate the validity and weight of our conclusion: Whatever the method of financing it might be, the economic benefits of scientific and industrial research can be exploited fully only if no one, no one at all, is prevented from using its results by the price which he has to pay to do so.

Exclusive possession of manufacturing know-how now seems to play a role as great as, or even greater than, formal patent rights. Not only the development of new products, but the methods employed to make these products depend more and more on the results of industrial research. By keeping these processes—or at least some of their essential stages—under cover, the enterprise that has developed them can attain the same ends that formerly would have required taking out (and possibly defending at great expense) a patent on the finished product.

A typical licensing arrangement nowadays covers not only the design but also detailed practical information on the methods of making the new product. Having spent large sums on developing the manufacturing know-how, a private firm cannot be expected to yield such information without charge. The resulting restriction in the application of new ideas in this case too inevitably leads, however, to retardation of technological progress and economic loss.

A telling example of productivity increase that can, in the long run, be brought about by absolutely free access to a steady flow of advanced technical ideas is offered by American agriculture. Traditionally, the bulk of agricultural research in this country was financed by Federal funds, and its results were put at the disposal of the potential users free of charge. In consequence, agricultural productivity has been increasing by leaps and bounds, finally even creating a glut of cotton and wheat.

As Dexter Keezer's statistics in the Appendix show, in the United States at the present time 60 per cent of research and development activities are financed by the government, and presumably some applications are permitted free of charge. The other 40 per cent are conducted on a commercial basis; the costs of the technical advance resulting from such privately financed research are covered by license fees or an equivalent markup included in the price of the new or improved goods. This means that practical application of many of the path-breaking discoveries of recent years is necessarily restricted. In an era in which economic progress depends so much on scientific research, such chronic underemployment of technical knowledge might have, in the long run, an even more deleterious effect on the rate of economic growth than idle capital or unemployed labor.

In conclusion I would like to state that, although the striking image of the research revolution presented in this book has influenced greatly what I have to say about the economics of invention, its author of course bears no responsibility for the above remarks.

Wassily Leontief

1

The Need to Grow

The American economy, in the years ahead, must grow at a strong rate or suffer some highly unpleasant consequences. Some of these are obvious, some less so.

The United States population is growing at an annual rate of 1.7 per cent per year, compounded. At present that means an annual increase of 3 million people—each year we grow by more than one Los Angeles. At that rate of growth the American population, now almost 180 million, will reach 300 million in just thirty years (in the last thirty, despite one decade of depression, we added 56 million to the population). With that in prospect, we are going to have to run pretty fast just to stay in the same place in terms of income per capita, just to prevent living standards from declining.

Unemployment

Without strong and sustained economic growth, the United States will have a serious and continuing unemployment problem on its hands, for the labor force is also growing rapidly. In the last decade the labor force has been growing by some 800,000 each year. But now we have, coming on in a rush, the enormous crop of war and postwar babies; they have been making our educational system burst at the seams in the 1950s and are just starting to enter the labor force. In the 1960s, the schools and colleges will be more crowded than ever, but the labor force will be growing by 1.1 million a year from 1960 through 1965, by 1.4 million a year from then through 1970. With more and more efficient machinery—with increasing automation in industries that have been big labor users—will there be work enough for all the extra hands?

Social-economic conflict

Too slow growth would mean a sharper battle over the shares of the national income going to labor, management, farmers, shareholders, and property owners. That would probably lead to more direct government intervention to control the intensified conflict and to determine who gets what. When total national income is growing faster than population, there is less occasion for conflict over how much each group gets, because all groups are either going forward or, at worst, holding their ground. Without such growth in national income, each group can advance its interest and enlarge its take only by damaging the interest—reducing the income share—of others.

Clearly, labor and other lower-income groups aren't content to settle for their present income level and standards of living. Labor's pressure for rising wages is certain to continue. Unless the rate of growth is at least equal to the rate of population increase plus the rate at which wages are pushed up, the consequences must be either inflation or a reduced return to capital—or both.

Money disillusion

The inflationists have been driven to cover, however, for reasons both domestic and international. American labor and other groups are no longer so bedazzled by a "money illusion," a belief that more money in the pay envelope automatically means that much more food, clothing, housing, or services. There's greater realization that an increase in money wages or incomes is worthless if prices rise, too, and the new wages buy no more than the old. At the same time, American businessmen have been learning that, with industrial capacity more ample than in the earlier postwar period and with competition more intense, it can be dangerously bad business to boost prices.

Internationally, the position of the United States in the world, both as banker and trader, makes inflation self-defeating. The United States is in a balance-of-payments bind, has had a rather rapid and persistent loss of its gold reserves. Further inflation would make American exports less competitive, aggravate the balance-of-payments problem, possibly set off a flight from the dollar, and breed an international financial crisis.

Moribund capitalism

But if the United States accepts "the discipline of the balance of payments," keeps interest rates high, keeps a lid on inflation—and at the same time there is not a strong national economic growth—then any attempt to accommodate labor's demands for higher real income and rising living standards would mean cutting the return to capital. This could mean, too, a cut in capital investment within the United States economy. Such a fall in investment would hold back United States growth still further. Government would be driven to step in deeper and deeper, both to resolve the conflict over income shares and to ensure that the fall in private investment did not bring heavy unemployment in its train.

Communist threat

Finally, too slow United States growth would mean that the Soviet Union might succeed in its bid to achieve world domination through its own growing economic power.

The shock of our lives has been the realization that a

political-economic system hostile to our own—a totalitarian system that most Americans, including the economists, thought was bound to limp along in a mess of inefficiency and bureaucracy—has proved capable of mobilizing its human and material resources to produce a strong and growing economy. In recent years, the Soviet economy has been growing faster than our own, twice as fast or even more. The Soviet leaders have been making powerful propaganda of that, directed particularly toward the world's poor nations, those that are determined to reduce the misery of their people.

That psychological, or "demonstration," war—which uses not only economic statistics but also space vehicles and itinerant composers, dancers, and professors to persuade the world that the future lies with communism—is important in its own right.

But the competition in economic growth is more than a war of numbers. For the real resources generated by the Soviets' growing economy have enabled them to build the scientific, military, and foreign-assistance programs that lie at the heart of the twentieth-century power struggle.

Underdeveloped nations

Even if there were no East-West conflict—with the poor nations of Asia, Africa, and Latin America among the major theaters of that contest—there would still be the so-called North-South problem. A strong and growing America can play the part of friend—both as capital ex-

porter and major customer—to the underdeveloped nations of the South; a stagnating America would far more
likely frustrate or antagonize the poor nations, breed even
greater troubles than we have already seen in this hemi-
sphere and in Africa and Asia.

For all these reasons, which touch virtually every aspect of our domestic and international problems, the
growth potential and performance of the American economy have become a crucial national issue.

New element in growth process

As this issue takes an unprecedented place in the political spotlight, a new element is becoming apparent in the
growth process itself—one that's destined to have a powerful impact on the pace of economic growth in the future
and, even more than that, on the structure of our society
and the nature of our civilization.

That element, largely a postwar phenomenon but with
roots that go back to the first industrial revolution, is industry's new understanding of the importance of regular,
systematic investment in scientific research and development.

This principle and practice of making regular provision
for the discovery and development of many new ideas,
new things, is taking increasing hold in American business, though its use still varies widely from industry to
industry. It is already an important factor; and in the
future it is likely to provide the spur to growth that came
in earlier periods from particular developments such as

steam power, railroads, electricity, automobiles. In reality, this discovery of the process of discovery represents a new revolution, a deep-going extension of capitalism's growth process.

Capital investment represents consumption deferred in the interest of greater production later; and research and development carries the process one step further. It represents a charge against current production in the interests of greater investment—and greater productivity—later. This may be a qualitative change of the same order of importance as the development of the concept of capital itself.

But this dramatic, new element, though its broad outlines can be clearly seen, is in itself a complex development; and it becomes part of an even more complex growth picture.

2

What Is Growth? Why the Confusion?

Much of the confusion over the growth issue arises from the welter of apparently conflicting statistics that rival politicians and economists hurl at each other. In truth, any journeyman economist could produce to order a veritable zoo of growth rates, with specimens to please every partisan who would like to prove that the American economy is stagnating, or that it is growing as fast as ever, or faster than ever, or that it is lagging far behind the Russians, a little behind the Russians, or not behind them at all.

All these data have this in common: They are based on calculating the rate at which some series of numbers representing national output or income, or per capita output or income, is, or is not, increasing. What leads to the variety of results is this: Depending upon the starting point for your time series and its terminal date—together with the periods you pick for comparison with other countries— you may prove almost anything you like. Even small shifts of base and terminal years over a fairly long span of years can make a sizable difference in the calculated annual growth rates. For instance, from 1949 to 1957, gross national product at constant prices grew at a 4.2 per cent rate annually. If you shift the period ahead one year at each end, however, you find that from 1950 to 1958, GNP at constant prices grew by only 2.8 per cent annually—a one-third drop in the growth rate.

This is not to say that all such growth rates are meaningless—or that it's not necessary, at some point, to try to lay out the data in a way that will give a sharper and clearer guide to events and to policy than words alone can do. But before we start working with numbers, we ought to be reasonably sure we know what we are talking about, what it is that the numbers are supposed to describe.

Organic growth

To do that, we must go back to the growth concept in economics. And economic growth is one of the most slip-

Annual Average Growth Rates of the United States Economy, 1946–1959 [1]

(Per cent increases, starting year to terminal year, of GNP in 1954 dollars)

Starting year	Terminal year													
	1946	1947	1948	1949	1950	1951	1952	1953	1954	1955	1956	1957	1958	1959
1946		−0.1	−1.9	−1.2	3.0	3.9	3.8	3.9	3.2	3.7	3.6	3.4	2.9	3.2
1947			3.8	1.8	4.1	4.9	4.6	4.6	3.7	4.2	4.0	3.8	3.2	3.5
1948				−0.1	4.2	5.3	4.8	4.7	3.6	4.3	4.0	3.8	3.1	3.4
1949					8.7	8.1	6.5	6.0	4.4	5.0	4.6	4.2	3.5	3.8
1950						7.4	5.4	5.1	3.4	4.3	3.9	3.6	2.9	3.3
1951							3.4	3.9	2.0	3.5	3.2	3.0	2.2	2.8
1952								4.4	1.3	3.6	3.2	2.9	2.0	2.6
1953									−1.6	3.2	2.8	2.6	1.6	2.4
1954										8.1	5.1	4.0	2.4	3.2
1955											2.1	2.0	0.5	2.0
1956												1.8	−0.2	2.0
1957													−2.3	2.0
1958														7.0
1959														

[1] Compound rates of growth.

SOURCE: Department of Commerce

19

pery and elusive concepts in a very slippery, "soft" science.

The trouble arises from the fact that the concept of economic growth (like so many concepts in the social sciences) is really an analogy derived from the natural sciences—specifically, in this case, from biology. Years ago Simon Kuznets suggested that economists concerned with growth might get a better idea of what they were talking about if they took a closer look at the biological source of their analogy.[1]

Biological growth, according to the classic definition of D'Arcy Thompson, is "a process, indirectly resulting from chemical, osmotic, and other forces, by which material is introduced into the organism and transferred from one part of it to another." [2]

So economic growth ought to involve similar processes in economic organisms. But what is an economic organism? Clearly it's not the flow of goods and services that issue from the economy each year (or each day or hour). Rather it is the complex of people, factories, stores, farms and forests and rivers, dams, houses, banks, airports, autos, highways that produce the stream of goods and services.

If you wanted to take a picture of that economic organism growing, you ought to do it the way a cameraman takes a picture of a flower growing. He would show you that biological growth from the beginning—first of all,

[1] S. Kuznets, "Measurement of Economic Growth," *Economic Growth: A Symposium, The Journal of Economic History,* supplement 7, New York, 1947, p. 11.

[2] D'Arcy W. Thompson, *On Growth and Form,* Cambridge University Press, New York, 1942, p. 82.

the seed popping, the stem climbing out above ground and growing into the plant, then the bud forming and the flower bursting into bloom.

The picture of an economic organism growing would show you, similarly, the changes that come to a dynamic industrial area over the years—rail lines spreading, factories building, new and more complex industrial equipment coming along. It would show you, too, some of the changes in the economic actors—the multiplying population, the expanding cities, the changes in occupations of the people as industrialism advances, even the changes in the faces of the people.

Such a pictorial representation of the growth of an economic organism would tell a dramatic story, but a somewhat superficial one. It would show, quite effectively, the outer manifestations of growth. But it would not show the growth beneath the surface that has been making possible that outer transformation—the underlying growth in ideas. Recording the growth in ideas is an impossible job, obviously, for the photographer; it's just as impossible for the economic statistician.

To describe the changes in the economy as a whole—not just a single industrial area—it would be difficult enough to try to estimate numerically even the economy's changing surface. To do it, the economist would have to put dollar values on the changing stock of usable land, labor, and capital goods; and those values would be constantly changing because they could only be imputed from the current flow of goods and services that issued from

them. But even that would give you a means of determining the capital value only of those factors of production
currently in use; what would you do with factors standing
idle—with temporarily idle factories or with oil reserves
not yet tapped or college professors on leave of absence
to study in England? Admittedly, you might make some
extremely crude estimates by transferring current market
values to all known factors of production, physical and
human.

But to measure the value of the underlying growth of
ideas is quite impossible. At a given moment, the ideas
may exist in the separate minds of researchers who have not
found a way to link them to the ideas of other researchers.
The ideas might even be due for enormous productive application but still be locked up in the files of a great corporation that is not yet ready to make their move with
the new product or new process.

It will not do to torture the analogy between economic
and biological growth to illustrate the ways in which new
material is ingested by biological or economic organisms,
transferred throughout the organism, so that it becomes
enlarged. Nevertheless, there is one part of the analogy
that, I think, does deserve the greatest possible stress: That
is the basic distinction in both cases between growth of the
organism—in economics, the growth of the system's productive capacity in the deepest sense—and the mere growth
in its current rate of operation.

Just as a growing boy may, for a time, be sick and lie in

bed, doing nothing, but still be growing, so may a nation's economy be in a temporary recession, or even a long depression, and still be growing.

There are at least two examples in recent history that show just how much this distinction can mean.

The German phoenix

In World War II Germany was devastated by Allied bombing and ground fighting; the remaining German population, after the war, was embittered, demoralized. To anyone arriving in Berlin or Frankfort at the end of the war, as I did, from the air, it was like coming down onto the cliffs or cities of some dead planet: As far as your eye could reach, you took in this nightmare of shattered, hollow buildings, this shattered culture.

So it seemed. Yet only a few years later the new Germany had become the economic powerhouse of Europe— not merely what it was in 1939 before the war, but a still bigger and more powerful economy, crowded into a smaller space.

Everyone, including the economists, was astonished by the speed of that transformation from wreckage to powerhouse. "I always thought it was impossible for the German economy to recover," says Theodore Schultz, who served with Allied occupation authorities in Germany just after the war. But he adds, "We were dead wrong—British economists, American economists, and for that matter, Germans." They had all underestimated the real growth forces in West Germany. The plants and cities that had been destroyed, says Schultz, "... were really quite secondary, minor details remedied in very short order."

United States case: growth in depression

Was the German case something special? We can use American economic experience to show much the same thing. After the 1929 crash, the American economy stagnated for almost a decade of depression. In 1938 we were still producing less than in 1929.

But when war came and full employment was restored, did we go back only to the 1929 level? On the contrary, we far surpassed it. By 1942 the nation's real output had already risen one-third above the mark set at the end of the boom of the 1920s. In a great rush the nation made up for the decade of depression; almost overnight it climbed up to where it might have been if there had been no long depression.

It was indeed as though the economy had been "growing" through the years while it was functioning at so low a level of output and employment.

Measuring growth

This quick look at the resemblances between economic and biological growth should make it clear that it is quite impossible to put into numerical tables the underlying organic growth of an economy. So economists have had to settle for the next best thing—which is to use current measures of economic output or income and seek to derive long-term growth trends from these "performance" records. We do this on the assumption that there is some meaningful relationship between changes in output or income and changes in the capacity of the underlying economy. And that does seem to be the case—over the long run. Provided that the time period covered is long enough to cancel out swings in the business cycle and that the beginning and final dates of the period covered have nothing freakish about them (generally speaking, base and terminal dates should be in approximately the same phase of their respective business cycles), such time series are about the best means available of measuring economic growth.

Charts 1 through 4—labeled "growth reckoners" by staff economists of the Committee for Economic Development—help show the way current output, despite cyclical swings, keeps returning to a long-term trend. These charts are plotted on a semilogarithmic scale which makes a constant percentage increase show up, not as a rising curve (as it would on an arithmetic chart), but as a straight line pointing diagonally upward. In this way, the charts straighten out long-term growth trends, making it easier to appraise the short-term swings away from them.

Chart 1 presents one of these growth measurements—and raises an important question about just where we are right now on the growth line. It shows that gross national product, measured in constant dollars, was growing steadily at an annual average rate of 2.9 per cent from 1909 to 1957. But, in the postwar period, from 1947 to 1960, the climb

Chart 1. Real Gross National Product, 1910–1960

(Seasonally adjusted quarterly data at annual rates.)

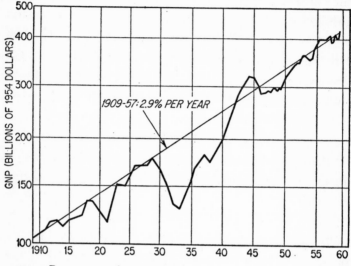

SOURCE: Department of Commerce

has been steeper: GNP has grown at the faster rate of 3.6 per cent a year.

Of course, if you take shorter periods within the postwar period, you can get some startlingly different results. From 1947 to early 1953, the growth rate of real GNP averaged almost 5 per cent. From mid-1953 to the first quarter of 1958, it was only a trifle better than 1 per cent a year. It is inevitable that such variations in "growth rates" should produce partisan political warfare. But partisan politics aside, the serious question the chart above raises is this: After a temporary postwar spurt, are we now back on the American economy's long-term 3 per cent growth trend?

Or have we started out on a new, postwar growth trend that is closer to 4 per cent? Or, indeed, does the chart suggest that a growth rate of 5 per cent per annum, attained during a part of this period, is in fact attainable in the future? Those who think so—including Governor Nelson A. Rockefeller of New York and Walter P. Reuther, president of the United Auto Workers—put major emphasis on the rising rate of productivity gains.

Chart 2. Real Gross National Product, 1947–1960

(Seasonally adjusted quarterly data at annual rates.)

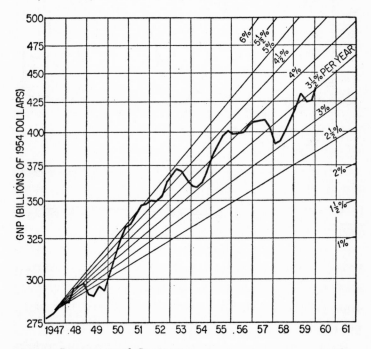

SOURCE: Department of Commerce

The postwar step-up in the rate of growth in total gross national product (which may or may not be slackening again) did not come about because the size of the work

Chart 3. Total Labor Force, 1947–1960

(Seasonally adjusted quarterly data.)

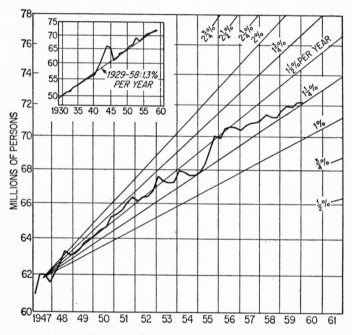

SOURCE: Census Bureau and Department of Labor

force has suddenly started to swell at a faster rate; since 1947 the labor force has been growing at just about the same pace as for decades—an average annual rate of 1.3 per cent.

Rather, the faster rate of postwar GNP growth has been

due to an apparently faster rate of increase in output per worker—as a glance at Chart 4 shows:

Chart 4. Real Gross National Product per Person
Engaged in Production, 1947–1960

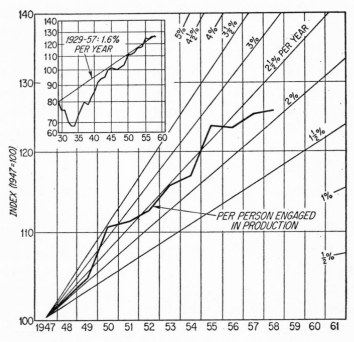

SOURCE: Department of Commerce

From 1929 to 1957, productivity (measured as real GNP per person engaged in production) has been edging up at an average rate of 1.6 per cent each year. Since 1947, the increase has speeded up to something close to a 2½ per cent rate.

Measuring productivity

But those are only one set of calculations of the rates of productivity increase—and you can get many different ones, depending on your definition of productivity: whether it is to include only labor inputs, or other factors of production, particularly capital, as well; whether it is calculated in terms of workers employed or, more appropriately, man-hours worked; whether you measure trends with straight lines or various kinds of mathematical curves, etc. The fact is that measuring productivity is one of the toughest, and most controversial, tasks an economic statistician can tackle.

The National Bureau of Economic Research, which prides itself on its scientific objectivity, finds evidence, however, to support the view that the rate of productivity gain has been increasing over the years. National Bureau economists have found that, during the quarter century before World War I, output per man-hour grew at a rate of 22 per cent per decade; since World War I, it has averaged 29 per cent per decade; and since World War II, growth in output per man-hour has stepped up to a rate of 35 per cent to 40 per cent per decade.

The National Bureau's research director, Solomon Fabricant, thinks it would be a mistake to assume from this that the pace of productivity gain will go on speeding up. On the contrary, he thinks it far more likely that there will be some slowdown in the rate of gains in the years just ahead; he bases this view on published work—and work in progress—by three National Bureau research associates: Simon Kuznets, John Kendrick, and Moses Abramovitz.

Their studies, covering nearly a century since the Civil War, suggest that changes in the rate of growth of productivity come in long cycles, lasting one to two decades. Periods of rapid gain centered in the late 1870s, the late 1890s, the early 1920s, the late 1930s, and the late 1940s or early 1950s. Periods of slower gain centered in the late 1880s, the late 1910s, the early 1930s, and the early 1940s (though the evidence for this period is somewhat confused because of the recovery from the Great Depression and the switch to war production).

This history suggests to Fabricant that we may be in for a long cyclical decline in the rate of productivity gains; this possibility disturbs him because of what it could mean for the pace of over-all American economic growth and the struggle with the Soviet Union, which, Fabricant finds on the basis of other National Bureau investigations, has been growing at a rate of 6 to 7 per cent a year, or about double the United States rate. National Bureau studies throw new light on what's behind those faster Soviet gains. They have not resulted from a faster climb in Soviet productivity; from 1928 to 1955, United States labor productivity rose about as rapidly as Russia's in terms of output per worker, and probably more rapidly in output per manhour. Over the twenty-seven years, Soviet productivity rose by 52 per cent, but with the steepest rise—21 per cent in output per worker—bunched at the end of the period, from 1950 to 1955. This implies a gain of better than 40 per cent for the whole 1950 decade—equal to, or better than, the hot post-World War II American rate of productivity gain.

Soviet industrial growth

Over the long haul, the National Bureau studies suggest, the big boost for Soviet total output came instead from rising industrial employment. In the United States, employment in industry rose at about the same pace as labor productivity, but in Russia industrial employment rose much faster. Fabricant concludes that Russia's great gains in output came primarily from diversion of manpower from agriculture and other sectors to industry. He sees in this important implications for Soviet nonindustrial output—and for the future rate of Soviet industrial growth as the possibility of such transfers runs out.

Conflicting readings

But the data on both Soviet and American productivity obviously lend themselves to many varying interpretations, which can scarcely avoid being affected by the interest positions or biases of the interpreters—Soviet or American. For instance, comparisons of Soviet and American economic progress over the long run are made exceptionally problematical by the different possible interpretations of the drags to Soviet progress during the long years of civil war after World War I and the tremendous destruction and loss of life during World War II.

Interpretations of the American growth statistics and their future implications are no easier, no less controversial. For instance, some Americans, after studying the record, reach exactly the opposite conclusion from Fabricant's that the rate of productivity gain is very likely to slow down in the period just ahead. Walter Reuther (and his economic adviser, Nat Weinberg) contend that the rate of productivity increase will continue the rate of acceleration which has occurred during the past fifty years. Reuther notes that, according to one analysis prepared by the Bureau of Labor Statistics, the rate of productivity increase has accelerated by 0.06 per cent per year during the period 1909–1958.[3] At the beginning of that period the rate of productivity gain was 0.9 per cent annually; at the end of the fifty-year period, it was 3.9 per cent annually. Thus, says Reuther, the rate of productivity gain is probably now at 4 per cent per year; and since he believes the labor force will grow at a rate of 1.7 per cent per year in the coming decade, he holds that a 5 per cent growth rate is entirely feasible—and that you could have that 5 per cent rate and still reduce the average number of working hours. (Governor Rockefeller, using much the same logic, argues that we should not reduce the number of working hours, and thus we can achieve a 6 per cent growth rate, which would just about match the Russians.)

Reuther contended, in his letter to *The New York Times*, that this acceleration of the rate of productivity gain has been concealed from the public for political or

[3] Letter to *The New York Times*, May 4, 1960.

collective-bargaining reasons: "Unfortunately, political and collective bargaining controversies concerning economic growth led the Bureau of Labor Statistics to downgrade and obscure the significance of findings on the historic acceleration of the rate of productivity advance." But those findings, said Reuther, are "... crucially important to all who recognize the imperative necessity for an adequate rate of economic growth and who are therefore concerned with measuring performance against potential."

The Bureau of Labor Statistics, caught in the cross fire between labor and management representatives on its Business and Labor Advisory Research Councils, could only draw some carefully hedged and inconclusive findings:

> Since World War II, productivity of the total private United States economy has been growing faster than the 50-year average rate of gain.
>
> But this is not unique. Productivity also spurted faster than the long-term average during the 1920s and middle and late 1930s.
>
> There is some evidence that productivity has been improving at an accelerating rate over the 50-year period (as the National Bureau research suggests).
>
> But if you exclude agriculture and its spectacular postwar growth in productivity, it is doubtful whether there has been any acceleration.

However, the BLS report by no means sought to dismiss the acceleration thesis. BLS acknowledged that its findings were consistent with those of the National Bureau of Economic Research which, as we have seen, did conclude that the long-term rate of advance in output per man-hour had speeded up.

BLS found that, from 1947 through 1958, output per man-hour increased 39 per cent. In manufacturing, the productivity of production workers alone has been climbing at an average 3.7 per cent a year. If we include nonproduction workers in the computation, the figure drops to 2.9 per cent.

Much of the argument over the BLS report stems from the different possible ways of interpreting the same data mathematically. The increase in productivity can be shown in chart form either as a straight line or as a curve. BLS chose to present most of its productivity data in the straight-line method, which shows a constant, not an accelerating, rate of gain. It describes this approach as the "usual" method. But BLS does include a section showing mathematical derivations from which a curve can be plotted to show an accelerating rate; two types of curves —parabolas and hyperbolas—are presented.

A parabola—a curve that shows a rate of gain changing at a constant pace—works out to show a productivity increase of 3.9 per cent, in terms of man-hours actually worked (rather than man-hours of labor paid for, whether spent at work or not). This last figure is Walter Reuther's 3.9 per cent. It comes closest to supporting the argument that there has been a major break-through since the war —that productivity is now growing at the rate of almost 4 per cent a year, rather than its prewar 3 per cent or less.

But, BLS notes, different mathematical techniques give different results. Using a hyperbola—a curve in which the rate of gain does not increase indefinitely but eventually reaches an upper limit—BLS pegs the 1958 rate of productivity increase at 3.7 per cent.

Using the "usual" straight-line method, however, BLS finds only an average gain per year in output per man-hour of only 3.1 per cent from 1947 to 1958. In agriculture, the rate of gain in productivity was 6.2 per cent; in manufacturing, 2.9 per cent; and in other lines, only 2.3 per cent.

The simple fact is this (and it's a disturbing one for people who don't trust economists): There is no one "true" growth rate for productivity or any other time series. But this is not to say that numbers can't be useful as a representation of reality, if used in a knowledgeable and honest way. One must not succumb to the temptation to regard all growth statistics as a nonsensical numbers racket.

The reality behind the numbers

For, however difficult it is to produce the data and interpret it correctly, the reality of economic growth is still there. And the numbers, roughly but indisputably, tell us that America's real gross national product today is more than four times as great as it was fifty years ago; by implication our economic organism is four times as great, or thereabouts.

That enormous economic growth has been, beyond doubt, the prime element in America's swift rise to pre-eminent world power. And it is, of course, the source of

America's high standards of living, the highest in the world (if that is a point that one may note without meaning to be bombastic, materialistic, jingoistic, or conventionally wise).

Further, whatever the complexities of the numbers, it is also a fact that, if we can sustain our high rate of productivity gain and at the same time maintain something like full employment of our growing labor force, future growth can be as dramatic, or more dramatic, than the growth which we have experienced in the past half century.

Obviously, it makes an enormous difference to the future of the United States which of the many possible growth rates you can derive from our historical experience is the valid one for forecasting. If we grow at only a 3 per cent rate in the years ahead—roughly our long-term average—real GNP will rise from approximately $500 billion in 1960 to $750 billion in 1975. If we achieve Governor Rockefeller's or Mr. Reuther's 5 per cent growth rate, real GNP in 1975 would top 1 trillion dollars. But if we don't succeed in getting anything better than a 2 per cent growth rate annually, population increase will very likely gobble up practically all of the gains—and increases in productivity at anything like their recent rate will mean unpleasantly high and chronic unemployment.

None of these possibilities is going to be determined by what happened in economic history; and achieving any growth rate obviously involves something more than laying a ruler on a trend line and pointing to the year you want, or selecting a nice figure for the compound rate of annual productivity increase and multiplying it by the future labor force, the number of hours they are likely to work, and the number of years for growing.

Such projections have their uses for government or business planning, or for propaganda, or for gee-whiz newspaper and magazine articles. But they tell you nothing about what *causes* growth. Data on rates of productivity increase tell you nothing about what made productivity rise; they only invite you to find out. Continuous economic growth—what Rostow likes to call "compound interest" —is not automatic; economies don't simply expand at rates of interest like money in the savings bank. Indeed, when you stop to think of it, money in the bank—no matter what the stated interest rate—doesn't automatically earn interest, either. Somebody has to figure out ways to make that money produce, or the bank will fail.

Explaining compound interest—for a bank or a nation —is the central problem of economics.

3

The Forces of Growth

What are the real forces that determine the growth of the economy? And to what extent can they be altered?

Scraps of various theories of economic growth have been littering our libraries for hundreds of years. But, after the middle of the nineteenth century, respectable economists abandoned the effort to understand growth and instead tried to turn economics into a neat, precise, deductive science like Newtonian physics. Growth was too messy

—too full of historical, sociological, technological, political, geographical, "institutional" complexities.

The gold rush into the growth field by economists after World War II started theories of growth multiplying again. The rush was spurred on by political factors—first, the drive of the poor nations for economic development and, second, the great thrust forward of the Soviet Union and the evolving competition between communism and capitalism. Its result has been the rediscovery of what the earlier writers, philosophers, historians, sociologists, and the classical economists had already learned.

This was that there are two basic sets of causes of growth:

One is the complex of cultural factors—including science, technology, population changes, religion, politics, social attitudes, class structure, and the intellectual and moral qualities of men: their skills, their imaginations, their drive, their courage.

The other is a set of economic factors—especially the possibility of accumulating capital and using it to make a profit.

These two sets of factors, cultural and economic, must conjoin if growth is to occur. The two come together in the act of investment; that is the genetic moment for economic growth.

What's more, there is a close and direct link between the rate of investment and the rate of economic growth. In the United Kingdom between 1950 and 1957, for example, gross investment stood at something over 13 per cent of gross national product, and the annual rate of increase in GNP was below 3 per cent. In Mexico, the United States, France, and Belgium, gross investment ran higher —between 16 and 17 per cent of GNP; and in these countries GNP climbed at rates varying from just over 3 per cent to just over 5 per cent. In Japan, Venezuela, and the Soviet Union, on the other hand, gross investment reached such expansive rates as 25 to 29 per cent of GNP; and the growth of GNP speeded up accordingly, ranging up to an 8 per cent rate in Japan and above 9 per cent in Venezuela. The correlation between rates of investment and rates of economic growth are by no means tight and consistent, but that there is an important causal link no economist would deny.

But if it is investment that plays so basic a role in economic growth, what causes investment to rise—or to sink?

Autonomous and induced investment

Broadly, in considering what spurs on the investment process, economists have come to split investment into two categories—autonomous investment and induced investment. Economists use both terms without much precision. What they mean approximately, though, is this:

Investment is autonomous when it creates its own demand.

Investment is induced when it represents a response to preexisting demand that forces producers to increase capacity.

Another way of putting the difference would be to say that autonomous investment results primarily from non-economic causes, from forces outside the economic system itself—that is, from the action of the various cultural forces that help to bring about economic growth.

Induced investment, by contrast, results primarily from economic factors—from changes in business activity, from the relationship of costs, prices, interest rates, profit margins, the ratios between sales and capacity, and other forces within the economic system itself.

Autonomous investment—which, as we shall see, is the heart of the long-term growth problem—comes chiefly from:

• The discovery of new techniques of production, such as the assembly line or the steam shovel; these cut production costs.

• The development of new products, such as the automobile or the television set; these create new markets.

• The development of new resources, such as petroleum or helium—a process usually stimulated by some technological advance (though at one time military conquest or exploration of distant lands played the leading role in bringing new resources to a nation's economy).

• Population growth and migration, which may stimulate investment in housing, public utilities, "social capital."

• War—hot or cold—which necessitates expansion of plant and equipment to produce defense goods or, for that matter in this age of total military, economic, diplomatic, psychological, foreign-aid competition, many other kinds of goods.

The last two factors—population growth and migration and war—may seem to come close to induced investment, or response to existing demands. But, essentially, they are noneconomic factors—"cultural" forces outside the operation of the economic system itself, and so are grouped with autonomous investment.

War and babies

As growth producers, however, both population increase and military requirements are uncertain in their effect. Certain military expenditures, for example, may clearly produce growth—such as expenditures for electronic research. Others may simply divert savings into stagnant channels, such as provision of barracks for troops. Considering the role of external threat on national development historically, Everett E. Hagen [1] concludes that such a military threat to a nation may be a powerful force toward economic growth, especially if it is combined with internal forces that are pushing a nation toward technological development. Hagen thinks this combination of internal and external pressures, for instance, accounts for the rapid transformation of Japan from stagnation to continuous growth.

Like Hagen, the ancients put great stress on threats of

[1] Everett E. Hagen, *An Analytical Model of the Transition to Economic Growth*, M.I.T. Center for International Studies, Document C/57-12.

enemies—or of nature—as a means of developing the powers of a people. Lucretius, for instance, thought storms, earthquakes, pestilences were necessary for the development of great national qualities. A couple of millennia later, that eminent English economist Alfred Marshall decided that the productivity and tone of English industry owed much to "... the natural gravity and intrepidity of the stern races that had settled on the shores of England...." Yet it should be perfectly obvious that combat or the natural intrepidity of peoples cannot be considered a sufficient cause of economic growth: Consider the pugnacious Zulus, Swahili, Apaches, etc.

The impact of population increase on economic growth is no more simple and direct than that of military threats. To most businessmen, of course, a fast-growing population seems unquestionably wonderful—a stimulus to the growth of sales, to profits, to investment. Businessmen greet as bad news word that, because we let the birth rate fall two decades ago during the Depression, a lower family-formation rate is now upon us. They look forward eagerly to the days, soon to come, when the postwar bumper crop of children come of marrying age and will begin to order more houses, bath tubs, baby buggies.

But to many an economist (especially those in countries like India), geochemist, biologist, or conservationist, rapid population growth is the bane of economic progress. Is population growth stimulative of economic growth in the United States, destructive in India?

The founding father of the worrisome view on population growth was of course T. R. Malthus, the English clergyman-economist, who held that population tended to grow geometrically, while resources increased only arithmetically. So, as limited resources were more intensively used, diminishing returns would set in, and per capita income would keep slipping below the starvation level, thereby restoring the balance between resources and people (just about at the starvation level).

Obviously, Malthus was too gloomy. Since his *Essay on Population* was published in 1800, world population has trebled; and, certainly in the Western world, living standards have risen enormously. The Malthusian devil retreated before the onrush of modern technology. Malthus's fundamental error was in regarding resources as relatively fixed—not, as they really are, a function of changing technology. As the demographer Raymond Pearl has said, Malthus's sad predictions seemed "... comically absurd soon after he made them."

In fact, only two decades ago, most Western economists were much more worried about what we might call the Malthusian angel—the prospect of population decline. For, in the 1930s in Western nations, the falling birth rate and falling national incomes seemed causally connected, and the cause-effect chain was held to run from population decline to income decline.

An outstanding proponent of this theory was the Swedish economist, Gunnar Myrdal, who argued that the worst effect of a shrinking population was that it dries up investment opportunities and creates wasteful imbalances in an economy's capital structure. For instance, Myrdal asked, what happens if capitalists make a mistake and build too many of the wrong kind of apartments in a growing city? Nothing serious—because, as the city's population continues to expand, customers will at length show up to rent the temporarily surplus apartments. But, if the city's population were shrinking, nobody would ever occupy them, and capital would be indefinitely tied up in useless property.

The same holds for the economy at large, said Myrdal. A shrinking population multiplies investment risks. A growing population, a growing market, he concluded, is the basic condition of a free, unregulated capitalist system. Still worse, the then-young Myrdal added, a declining population is an aging population—and such a society tends to become a gerontocracy, suffers a loss of vigor and opportunity.

Myrdal's case was powerfully impressive to a world worrying about social decay, economic stagnation—and the threat of world war, for which large numbers might mean national survival. Myrdal's argument, and others like it which were heard in other countries, helped lead governments to adopt "population policies" aimed at stimulating the birth rate by such devices as housing subsidies and family allowances.

To many, the postwar boom we have had in both population and income has appeared further to confirm the Myrdal position. Since World War II, many American companies have based their expansion plans essentially on

population forecasts, taking for granted the positive correlation between rising population and rising national
income.

But a growing number of economists think this is a
phony assumption. Some, such as Joseph J. Spengler of
Duke University, in fact argue that population growth
actually depresses income. The antipopulation case is this:

Population growth does create a *need* for more investment (if a nation is to maintain present living standards),
but it does not necessarily create an effective *demand,* in
the economic sense. For instance, increasing numbers of
people in India or Thailand may need more housing—but
what they may effectively demand is more mud huts or
more sidewalk space on city streets. Even in advanced
countries, more people may effectively demand more housing—but at the expense of the investment that would
raise per capita output and income. The notion that you
need more people to stimulate investment to create more
jobs for more people seems, to antipopulation economists,
"pecuniary logic gone mad."

A growing population, they point out, reduces the relative size of the age group (say eighteen to sixty-five years
old), who actually produce income, increases the part of
the population who must be supported. The American
population, because of a simultaneous rise in the birth
rate and decline in the death rate, is in fact growing fastest at both ends of the age-distribution—thus providing
double burdens for the working people in the middle.

Population growth is already pressing hard against certain scarce United States resources, depressing income in hard-to-measure ways. It is draining away our water supply, creating serious water shortages in many areas. It is breeding serious problems of congestion, requiring enormously expensive capital expenditures (on highways, bridges, tunnels, airports, etc.) to remedy. It is causing air pollution, gobbling up clean and pleasant country and beach land. It is causing us to waste a frightful amount of time—and temper—commuting. As time goes on, growing population will press still harder against domestic and world supplies of minerals and fossil fuels, push raw material costs higher.

A rising population is no guarantee against economic depression: The depressions of the nineteenth century certainly occurred in the midst of rapidly rising population movements. In fact, the cause-effect relation really runs the other way: Higher income causes a higher birth rate (though this relation is not invariant). The anti-population-growth school does concede that a growing population does stimulate certain kinds of investment, in high-income societies—such as investment in housing or schools—but they see no reason why a nation, in the absence of rapid population growth, cannot devote more of its income either to other forms of investment (that might be more productive of growth than investment in housing) or to raising consumption levels.

But the answer to the riddle of whether population growth is economically desirable or undesirable depends on some factual questions the answers to which will vary from nation to nation, and from time period to time period: Will increasing population permit better utilization of existing resources? Will it be a spur to technological progress? (Will, in other words, the necessity of coping with larger populations, in fact mother inventions which will more than deal with the problem—which will raise per capita income?) Is the economy flexible enough to adjust to downward shifts in the rate of population growth, or even to population decline? Can the greater risks to capital be offset by compensating government policies?

The fundamental welfare question, of course, is whether technological progress will keep usable resources growing faster than numbers of people. Possibly, even the living-space problem could be solved technologically—by emigration to the moon or to other planets. The question of why earthlings would want to populate outer space is obviously beyond the realm of demography or economics.

A nicely hedged conclusion about the effects of population pressure—or military threats—is about as far as I would go: Neither is necessarily a stimulus to economic growth; neither is necessarily a drag. Both may be either.

The power of new ideas

What does become increasingly clear is that the most important element in autonomous investment (whether sparked by population pressure, military dangers, idle curiosity, the instinct of workmanship, or the love of a dollar) is the growth of scientific and technological knowledge which culminates in new products, new processes, new resources—in other words, innovational investment. There we find the great progenitor of economic growth.

In the past, the United States has had three great innovational pushes that have sent the economy climbing upward, each lasting about half a century. The first big push—based on cotton textiles, iron, and steam power— lasted from the end of the American Revolution until the 1840s. Then came the second push—based on the building of the railroads, and on steel—lasting until close to the end of the 1890s. The third thrust—powered by electricity and the automobile—got under way around the turn of the century, probably ended a few years ago.

It is going to be a lot harder, though, to fasten a label on the new innovational push that we have been experiencing since the end of World War II. That's because it has not been based on any one or two innovations that provide a convenient tag, but upon a whole flood of them.

These postwar innovations owe their origin to major scientific progress in nuclear and solid-state physics, organic and inorganic chemistry, electronics, engineering, the earth sciences, the biological sciences, mathematics. The important scientific work that led to break-throughs —and innovations—in those fields stretched back through the war years and on through the years of apparent economic stagnation in the 1930s (when the work of scientists such as Einstein, Lawrence, Fermi, and Meitner was far from stagnating).

What will this new epoch be called? It's clearly an understatement to call it the atomic age, as people did at the end of the war. It's too narrow to call it the age of automation or cybernetics, as Norbert Weiner did. And it's much more than the space age. Because of its tremendous breadth, we might simply call it the research age, however vague the term, however subject to misuse.

There are almost as many interpretations of the term *research* as there are people who can pronounce the word. To the man in the street, research may just be a synonym for progress, for something good. To the broker in Wall Street, it may just be a sales gimmick. To the pure scientist, it means exploring the unknown. He's looking for truth, or for information or relationships, if you prefer less exalted language—not to solve any particular problem, but for the sake of knowing.

New products and processes, the tangible aspects of progress and a higher standard of living (or a more potent nation) clearly derive from discoveries of the pure scientist. But there's a wide middle ground between pure research and the creation of new products; and it's this middle ground that is constantly under fire. Out of this area, observers have carved segments known as basic research, fundamental research, applied research, process development, and product development. The main line of demarcation of course is supposed to be the one that separates pure from applied research. Some people who have lived on both sides of that border are beginning to take a philosophical view. Money is much more readily available for applied research than for pure research. So many scientists frequently tell you that it is much simpler to go ahead and do the work, calling it applied, than it is to explain to the man guarding the money that the additional equipment or personnel are really for pure research, the results of which can't be imagined.

This research revolution has happened so fast that it's hard to see it in perspective, to be sure that one isn't either exaggerating or underestimating the dimensions of the revolution. Science and technology now play so prominent a role in everyday life and in our business affairs that it seems inconceivable that only 400 years ago people shied away from Galileo and considered him a practitioner of the black art. Some scholars see the application of science and technology to industry as having come on in three stages. It is hard to find accurate tags for the stages, since they shade into one another. They might perhaps be called the stages of (1) the isolated inventor, (2) the organized investigators, and (3) the organized scientists.

1. Man had been inventive since the beginning of time, but not until he had collected a great deal of information about nature and perfected his processes of reasoning did he become "scientific." When inventors began to use the scientific method in the eighteenth century, the result was the industrial revolution. Large-scale mechanical manufacturing, which started in Britain, spread technology around the world. In this country, whole new industries sprang up from the inventions of such men as Eli Whitney, Robert Fulton, Elias Howe, Samuel F. B. Morse, Cyrus McCormick, Alexander Graham Bell, Charles Goodyear, John Wesley Hyatt, Thomas A. Edison, Charles M.

Hall. The pace of inventing had enormously quickened in the nineteenth century from earlier periods. Alfred North Whitehead has put the matter this way: [2]

> What is peculiar and new to the [nineteenth] century, differentiating it from its predecessors, is its technology. It was not merely the introduction of some great isolated inventions. It is impossible not to feel that something more than that was involved. For example, writing was a greater invention than the steam-engine. But in tracing the continuous history of the growth of writing we find an immense difference from that of the steam-engine. We must, of course, put aside minor and sporadic anticipations of both; and confine attention to the periods of their effective elaboration. For scale of time is so absolutely disparate. For the steam-engine, we may give about a hundred years; for writing, the time period is of the order of a thousand years. Further, when writing was finally popularized, the world was not then expecting the next step in technology. The process of change was slow, unconscious, and unexpected.
>
> In the nineteenth century, the process became quick, conscious, and expected. . . . The greatest invention of the nineteenth century was the invention of the method of invention.

2. But, though the method of invention was known, and the pace of inventions had greatly accelerated, the great technological contributors of the nineteenth century were mainly isolated geniuses who may themselves have known relatively little about science. In Germany, toward

[2] Alfred North Whitehead, *Science and the Modern World*, The Macmillan Company, New York, 1946, pp. 140–141.

the end of the nineteenth century, a second phase in the application of science to industry began. With a push from the Kaiser in the form of institutes, German science was encouraged to correct and enrich industrial processes. This was the beginning of organized research. The American effort in this second phase was slow in starting, because natural resources here were so plentiful that the idea of conservation or technological development of resources seemed rather unimportant. But the effort did begin at length in the laboratories of Arthur D. Little (1886), Eastman Kodak (1893), B. F. Goodrich (1895), General Electric Co. (1900), National Bureau of Standards (1901), E. I. du Pont de Nemours & Company (1902). By 1920, the number of such organized research laboratories was only 220. But during the 1920s and 1930s, we outstripped all competition in the organized application of science to manufacturing.

3. The third phase—in which basic science is emerging as the initiator and leader of industrial practice—is the astonishing one which has broken upon us, most obviously, since World War II, though its roots extend further back in time. The British scientist and novelist C. P. Snow observes [3] that this new phase is certainly related to the great industrial revolution of the eighteenth to the early twentieth century, but he finds it ". . . far more deeply scientific, far quicker, and probably far more prodigious in its result."

[3] C. P. Snow, *The Two Cultures and the Scientific Revolution,* Cambridge University Press, New York, 1959, p. 31.

This change comes from the application of real science to industry, no longer hit and miss, no longer the ideas of odd "inventors," but the real stuff.

Dating this second change is very largely a matter of taste. Some would prefer to go back to the first large-scale chemical or engineering industries, round about sixty years ago. For myself, I should put it much further on, not earlier than thirty to forty years ago—and as a rough definition, I should take the time when atomic particles were first made industrial use of. I believe the industrial society of electronics, atomic energy, automation, is in cardinal respects different in kind from any that has gone before, and will change the world much more.

Probably the greatest thing that sold industry on the new approach was the way organized research attacks paid off in World War II. By 1939 British scientists were moving into high places in their government and industry to attack a wide variety of problems. In this country the Office of Scientific Research and Development performed much the same function, and initiated many of the wonders that helped to win the war. Most dramatic and important of all was the Manhattan project, which enlisted and coordinated the talents of many specialists in the quest for the atom bomb. Here time was the vital element; there was no question about how badly we needed the atom bomb. We organized to get it, and we got it. Similarly, in the chemical industry, there was urgent need to find a way synthetically to replace natural rubber, and a search was organized. Everybody with any knowledge about polymers was invited in on this one; some of the big chemical companies donated the services of whole groups of researchers for $1 a year. Again the search was successful, and the United States was able to build enough rubber plants to ease its dependence on imported rubber during the war. With these and such other great technological achievements as radar and the antibiotics, one can go a long way toward supporting the thesis that war—at least World War II—has been a powerful propellant of economic development.

The revolution spreads

The research revolution has deepened and widened since the war. Nor is it only the big, sensational things—headline-grabbers such as atomic reactors, hydrogen bombs, electronic computers, jet transports, atomic submarines, earth satellites—that have issued forth from this new innovational push. The list of new products that have staged a fast growth in the postwar period is long. Here are just some of the fastest-growing new products and new services, spawned by industrial research and development, that have helped push the economy upward at a rapid pace in the 1948–1958 decade:

Products with growth rates of 40 per cent per year—or more:

> Transistors
> Titanium sponge
> Power steering
> Power brakes
> Antibiotics

Television sets
Polyethylene
Styrene plastics and resins
Vitamins
Helicopters (nonmilitary)
Synthetic rubber
Butadiene
Synthetic detergents

Products with growth rates of 30 to 40 per cent per year:

Television broadcasting stations
Ton-miles of air flown
Synthetic fibers (except rayon)
Electric driers
Automatic coffee makers
Argon
Room air conditioners
Tape recorders
Pentaerythritol

Products with growth rates of 20 to 30 per cent per year:

Tractors
Polyvinyl resins
Passenger-miles of air flown
Pickup hay balers
Electric blankets
Helium
Rayon and nylon cord
DDT
Synthetic ammonium sulfate

You could go on and on—through the roster of 15 to 20 per cent per year growers (diesel locomotives, food disposal units, automatic transmissions, trailer coaches, frozen foods), and the 10 to 15 per cent per year class (home freezers, sulfa drugs, automatic dishwashers, transparent film for packaging, synthetic ammonia), and so on. The impact of product and process innovation is obvious throughout the roll call.

There's another side to this picture, however. You find it in the list of products that have shown a declining trend through the postwar period. Lumped together in this group are sheepskins, local transit, lead, cast-iron boilers, railroad passenger cars, anthracite coal, radiators and convectors, steam locomotives, tin, brick, woolen goods, tractor moldboard plows, work shirts, domestic heating stoves, creamery butter, black blasting powder, natural soap, textile bags—and other victims of technological change.

Many of these declining products represented innovations in their day (if you go back far enough, all of them did). And like them, each of the multitude of postwar innovations has its own life to live. Some will have a long and pretty steady period of expansion before they taper off. Others shoot up like a rocket, hit a ceiling, then perhaps drop back. Still others will keep booming upward for a long time.

This falling off of obsolescent products as technology changes is the reverse side of the innovation process on which the late Joseph Schumpeter built his theory of economic growth and business cycles. It is what Schumpeter called "creative destruction"—creative, because the ultimate effect of innovation is growth, not stagnation; capitalism is a system of economic change that, in his words, ". . . not only never is but never can be stationary." [4]

This process of growth via technological progress and innovation is, of course, nothing new; long before Schumpeter, the early eighteenth-century Canadian economist John Rae—Adam Smith's foremost critic—built a theory of growth based on technological change and industrial innovation. And, economic theory apart, technological progress has played a major role in propelling this economy, and other economies, forward, particularly since the middle of the eighteenth century.

But what is new in our time is the multiplication of innovations—and the widespread recognition and systematic application by industry of the notion that new products and new processes are the key to a company's growth, an industry's growth, a nation's growth—and the recognition that, through systematically planned and administered research, we can count on the continuous development of innovations to keep the economic system expanding.

We do not know precisely what our laboratories will discover in the years ahead. But we do know that if we sponsor an adequate research program, they will make discoveries that call for new investment and generate greater production. Knowing this, we can, in a real sense, make innovation a deliberate program rather than a chance development and thus ensure future growth.

[4] J. A. Schumpeter, *Capitalism, Socialism and Democracy*, Harper & Brothers, New York, 1942, p. 82.

4

The Case of Transistors

For a case study in the new research revolution, consider the tiny transistor.

In 1948, a team of physicists at Bell Telephone Laboratories tossed some dice to electronics manufacturers and started a scramble the likes of which even that volatile industry had never seen. The dice were the first transistors —tiny chips of specially prepared germanium metal that demonstrated a new way to control and amplify electric signals, the most basic job performed by any kind of electronic equipment.

By 1960, transistors and kindred devices were selling at an annual $500 million clip, and there are predictions of a $1 billion rate by 1963. The business is popularly known as the semiconductor industry, because its products are made from semiconductors, a group of materials with electrical characteristics that can be tailored to control electric current in a particular way; the products themselves are often called semiconductors, too.

The first transistors launched a chain reaction of new products and technological discoveries that are making semiconductors the dominant force in the $10 billion electronics industry, and a significant force in the electrical-equipment field as well. Manufactured goods using semiconductor components, from midget portable radios to giant computers, are the biggest, fastest-growing segment of the market for new electronic equipment.

In only a dozen years, the semiconductor industry has accomplished enough to rank it, probably, as the world's fastest-growing big business. Not only that—it is an almost classic example of the particular kind of growth that technological innovation can stimulate throughout the national economy, the growth that can be achieved through systematic research and development, with results often far removed from the original R&D goals.

But having to depend on innovation for growth makes it tough for businessmen to chart a course. That is why the semiconductor industry, important and exciting in its own right, is also a meaningful case history for executives in any business and everyone else seeking an understanding of the new process of economic change.

Source of growth

The industry has another distinction in the way it grew. The technical knowledge for all its strides stems basically from the same source: *Mother Bell's Cookbook*. Bell Labs made its early findings about semiconductors readily accessible to outsiders, and fledgling companies were able to refine or add to Bell's recipes and make a lot of money fast from the improvements, before the competition caught on. This pattern of innovation, profit, imitation has made continuing innovation all the more vital to the young industry, and a number of companies have started from nothing and fattened by following it.

Before semiconductors came along, the electronic industry faced a crisis. In the words of Daniel Noble, executive vice-president of Motorola, Inc., ". . . equipment had to have so many components of limited reliability that the total system's reliability was zero—it wouldn't work." But, compared to the vacuum tubes that were frequently used in such systems, semiconductor components are cheap, small, simple, long-lasting, and much more reliable—at best, several magnitudes more so than all but the most expensive tubes.

Transistors, the best-known of these components, in 1959 accounted for slightly more than half of the industry's $400 million sales (up from $228 million in 1958).

Two other components approximately split the balance of 1959's semiconductor sales: rectifiers—devices that let current pass in one direction only and are most commonly used to convert alternating current to direct current—and diodes, which are low-power rectifiers used as one-way electrical gates at signal-power levels.

The military now gives the new industry about half of its sales income, and this market will continue to grow. A single missile may carry as many as 6,000 transistors, and its control equipment may contain tens of thousands more. On the civilian side, electronic controls are just beginning to open as a market. They are vital to computers, virtually all of which use semiconductor components. A small computer has one thousand or more transistors and several times as many diodes within its anatomy; a really big one may contain several hundred thousand such devices. Among consumer goods, all portable radios are transistorized, and transistorized table radios are gaining popularity. Portable transistorized television sets are in production, and standard television sets will probably switch to semiconductor parts when prices dip a little more. But the market has only started to grow.

The boom in semiconductors has often been likened to an earlier phenomenon in electronics: the excitement that followed the discovery of the vacuum tube. But the analogy is inexact. True, most transistors still do jobs similar to those assigned to vacuum tubes. A transistor radio looks just like a tube radio in miniature. Because of transistors' virtues of small size and low power drain, they have been substituted for tubes wherever costs and technical factors permit. And this change has opened a market that enabled transistor makers to move quickly into high-volume operations yielding profits to finance the really revolutionary developments just now taking shape.

But transistors are not tubes. The resemblance ends with the similarity of certain jobs both can do. In ten years, transistors duplicated the first forty years of the vacuum tube's growth. There is practically no replacement market for transistors, since they seldom wear out; replacements account for something approaching half of tube sales. Transistors work differently, and they are set up on different types of circuits. And it takes different technologies to produce transistors and tubes.

Perhaps the most striking evidence of the gulf between transistors and tubes is that the nation's first and second biggest makers of semiconductor devices—Texas Instruments, Inc., and Transitron Electronic Corp.—attained their leads without ever turning out a tube. And although most major tube manufacturers at the outset made and marketed semiconductor devices within their tube divisions, they soon suffered some severe cases of indigestion. As a result, such companies as General Electric, RCA, Raytheon, and Sylvania have divorced the two and set up completely autonomous semiconductor operations.

Although transistors and tubes can do some of the same jobs, a transistor is a strikingly different item. Transistors and other semiconductor devices can tackle tasks that require many thousands of units in one system. Such jobs would be utterly impractical with tubes. Their talents are such that many scientists and engineers think the transistor ranks as one of man's greatest technological ideas.

Multiplying innovations

It's not hard to see why they think so. Without transistors, big computers would be impractical and uneconomic. Missile electronic control systems would be wholly impractical, unthinkable. With semiconductor devices, computers with the logical capacity of the human brain are not only possible—they are being built. Missile control systems are now being designed that can be stored three years or more and be ready instantaneously, with no failures and no warm-up time required. Huge systems of electronic controls are, for the first time, reliable enough to run a steel mill, a utility, or an entire chemical complex.

In time, semiconductor devices may do even more to revolutionize the electronic industry. One way they will do this is by eliminating interconnections—the points most likely to fail in a complicated electronic system. Some transistors are already more reliable than a soldered electrical connection between two copper wires. In time, semiconductors will transform a radio chassis from a collection of separate parts into a single solid chunk about the size of an after-dinner mint, containing many circuit elements combined in modular form with a minimum of interconnections. Westinghouse Electric Corp.'s semiconductor division has already contracted with the Air Force to design just such a communications receiver, and commercial versions will undoubtedly follow.

Circuits arranged in this way are often called circuit functions, or solid-state circuits. *Solid state* is a term sometimes used incorrectly as a synonym for semiconductors, but solid-state devices are any elements that can control current without moving parts, heated filaments, or vacuum gaps; all semiconductors are solid-state devices, but some solid-state devices, such as transformers, are not semiconductors.

Solid circuits will probably be cheap enough to throw away if one of the sealed segments goes bad. But failure will be much less likely than in the best of today's electronic devices, since there is nothing to wear out in transistors or in the circuits utilizing them.

The advent of solid circuits in quantity will upset some of the familiar marketing patterns in electronics. A computer maker will no longer buy a dozen or so different kinds of components—transistors, capacitors, resistors, and so on—from different manufacturers and then hook them together. Instead, he will be able to order a "bi-stable amplifier" or a "flip-flop circuit" ready-made in a package the size of one of today's transistors. The first commercial versions of such devices are already on the market.

These circuits are going to be vastly important, particularly in big computers and complex control systems. But semiconductors will be taking on other assignments, too, in fields such as refrigeration and power generation. As they become more and more adept at handling large

amounts of power, they will be controlling more big electric motors and doing other chores that take muscle as
well as speed.

With such prospects ahead, it is clear that the lightning
growth of the semiconductor industry has been no flash in
the pan. Although the first practical transistor appeared
twelve years ago, the semiconductor industry as such is
really only nine years old. It took three years to prepare
the components to graduate from the laboratories. In its
short life, the industry has attracted ninety-odd companies
in the United States, including all the integrated electronic
giants on the one hand and, on the other, small-scale speculative ventures, reminiscent of those that sprang up in the
early days of the vacuum tube. Of the ninety or so companies, only about thirty-five are significant producers; of
the rest, some are still working in the laboratory, some are
in pilot production, and some are very marginal operators.

There is no doubt that the industry will soon dwarf the
business of manufacturing vacuum tubes. But it is impossible to predict which of the ninety companies will survive,
or which will emerge on top. Already, some very solid
newcomers have appeared, including Texas Instruments
and Transitron, and it is a safe bet that they and the large
diversified electronic corporations will stay in the fore-
front.

Long on brains

Since they all lean so heavily on research, the companies
are all long on brains, short on brawn. It doesn't take

much capital to get into the business. And technical changes come so fast that it usually doesn't pay to invest heavily in plant and equipment; they would soon be obsolete.

The swift changes have another effect: Industry rankings are shuffled from week to week. And new products pour out in such a flood—hundreds a month at times—that technical-bulletin departments look like the city room of a daily newspaper.

So the best investment is in brains—in metallurgists, physicists, chemists, and, most sought after of all, in the rare hybrid scientists who can act as bridges between specialists in such diverse fields as crystal metallurgy, surface chemistry, electronic physics, and circuit design. Top management abounds in Ph.D.s.

The brains who run the semiconductor industry have had some pesky problems. The young giant is stumbling all over itself in a rush to expand. The most common sales tactic is the price cut (unit prices in any established line tend to fall a disconcerting 30 per cent a year), and it is fortunate for the marketing men that volume keeps climbing. Talent is scarce, and competitors continually raid each other's ranks. Limited funds for research and development have to be stretched over broad areas. Vested interests resist innovations. Even experts cannot hope to keep up with all developments in the field. On the fringes of the industry, the grapevine spreads misinformation wildly; the boom has attracted its share of job jumpers, fast-buck operators, unscrupulous promoters. Distasteful as this may be, it should not be permitted to obscure the powerful economic impact of this new industry—and the new process of organized research that mothered it.

Basic research builds an industry

Like many of science's recent achievements, the development of semiconductor devices was not the personal drama that led to, say, James Watts's steam engine. Instead, it was more akin to Du Pont's attack on polymer chemistry that created nylon and other synthetics. The transistor, like nylon, was the product of some basic, purposeful digging into the unknown—in this case, into the properties of semiconducting materials.

The search for the transistor was a race against time (like the race for the atomic bomb) to remove the greatest single threat to the Bell Telephone System. By the mid-1940s, that system was exploding in complexity and size. It was outgrowing the limits of components such as relays and electronic devices using conventional vacuum tubes. By switching from manual to automatic exchanges in the 1930s and 1940s, telephone companies had solved one labor and cost problem by eliminating central operators. But the new electromechanical monster needed many skilled, expensive maintenance crews to keep it running. The telephone company simply needed a new kind of switch—one that would not wear out and could be produced at reasonable cost.

The first step toward that goal, though no one realized it

at the time, was taken early in 1940 in the office of Mervin J. Kelly, then president of Bell Labs. Russell S. Ohl, a staff member working with silicon metal (one of the most common semiconductor materials), demonstrated an unusual photoelectric cell made from pure silicon.

Until that time, photocells had operated on the electrical effect produced by the interaction of the surfaces of two different metals exposed to light. Ohl's cell, by contrast, generated current in a single piece of metal—and the current was about ten times stronger than usual.

One of the witnesses at the demonstration, as it happened, was Walter H. Brattain. Sixteen years later, he and two fellow physicists—William O. Shockley and John Bardeen—received the Nobel prize for their work with transistors.

It took many years to build enough knowledge of semiconductors even to predict a device that could amplify or switch current. The research team at Bell Labs had to break unknown ground in metallurgy and chemical analysis and to do some abstruse theorizing in quantum mechanics.

The pieces of the puzzle suddenly fitted together in 1947. In November of that year, Bardeen and Brattain produced a low-frequency amplifier by immersing a piece of silicon in a salt solution. In doing so, they demonstrated a theory developed by Shockley on space charges. The next stride came only a month later, after the team had switched from silicon to germanium, another common semiconductor material, but one that is easier to handle. Brattain then noted the first amplifying, or "transistor," effect that existed in a solid semiconductor.

In June, 1948, the transistor made its official debut to the Bell Labs staff, the press, and the military.

The first devices were point-contact transistors, so-called because they consisted simply of two sharpened wires pressed into a piece of germanium. In the transistor's passive state, almost no current would flow through the germanium between the two pointed wires. But if a tiny current were introduced into the germanium by a third wire, the electrical resistance between the two point contacts would virtually disappear. Then a much larger current could conceivably flow between them.

This simple phenomenon is the basic magic of electronics: A small current can control a larger one. This process can go on in successive stages, almost as fast as a streak of light, until a tiny original signal has been multiplied millions or even billions of times and can do dozens of jobs—vibrating the cones of loudspeakers to produce sound or turning on a rocket motor or changing the direction of a missile far out in space.

The point-contact transistor was a partial answer to the need for a better switch. The device looked simple; it had no parts to wear out or burn out, and it was incredibly small. But, electrically and mechanically, it was weak and fragile. Its noise limited its use as an amplifier. It could do only a few of the jobs that were easy for vacuum tubes or relays, and this limited its applications.

Besides, Bell Labs' physicists didn't really understand why a point-contact transistor worked. Until the answer was found, production of the devices was doomed to remain a chancy business; some in a batch would work, some wouldn't, and no one knew why. It was doubtful whether high-volume, close-tolerance production was possible at all.

Nevertheless, point-contact transistors were produced. The good ones were selected and the bad ones thrown away. Only recently has this chancy method of production changed.

Despite its drawbacks, the point-contact transistor proved that a solid-state amplifier would work. The next advance required more basic research—this time into the properties of crystalline semiconductors and, with the help of mathematical theory, into the behavior of electrons in solids.

From the fruits of these studies, Shockley in 1949 was able to predict mathematically that it would be possible to produce a new type of transistor based on a single crystal of semiconductor material. (The point-contact devices were made from pieces of material with many crystals.) Instead of causing current to flow between two delicate wire points, Shockley proposed a method of controlling current flow between areas of impurity elements in the crystal itself. These impurities would be introduced into the single crystal in amounts so tiny that ordinary chemical or metallurgical analysis could not detect them. Scientist call the boundaries between differing impurity levels "junctions." Because the junctions would be relatively much bigger than the wire points in a point contact, a junction transistor could handle much more power, Shockley speculated.

Before Shockley's theory could be put to practice, more basic research was needed. Metallurgists and chemists had to find ways to make germanium purer than any material had ever been before. Impurities could make up no more than one part in a million or several in a billion. It was, as one scientist said, "like trying to separate a pinch of salt evenly distributed through a trainload of sugar when you didn't even know the impurity was salt."

Not until 1951 could the first junction transistor be made to work. But it still seemed doubtful that transistors ever could be built to fit predetermined specifications. Better materials were essential.

In 1954, almost unbelievably, Bell Labs came through with another break-through. William G. Pfann, a metallurgist, invented zone refining. This is a high-frequency heating technique that can melt a localized area of a long ingot of germanium, or other metal, and sweep the melted zone through the length of the ingot. The melted material is either a more or less effective solvent for impurities than the solid; so it sweeps the impurities in the metal to one end or the other of the crystal.

This technique was a boon: It not only purified the germanium, but it also concentrated the impurities in one end where more of them could be identified. It also provided a way to spread impurities evenly, under close controls, through the crystal. Thus, with vastly improved materials, the semiconductor industry was off to the races.

The sorcerer's apprentices

When the semiconductor industry began its growing, Bell Labs held basic design and process patents covering the entire field. The growth gained terrific impetus from Bell's policy of putting these virtually in the public domain. Almost 90 per cent of the semiconductor items now in commercial production came right out of *Mother Bell's Cookbook*.

One factor behind Bell's policy was the legal storm that has been swirling around electronics patents for years now and hasn't yet entirely subsided. Over the years, Department of Justice antitrust attorneys under both Republican and Democratic administrations have pretty well established it as a principle that, broadly, a company should not be allowed to use a patent monopoly as a weapon to dominate an industry.

In 1949, the antitrusters filed a suit seeking to separate American Telephone & Telegraph from its manufacturing arm, Western Electric, and dealing also with the Bell System's patents. Meanwhile, Western Electric offered to license all comers for its transistor patents on payment of a $25,000 advance royalty. J. A. Morton, vice-president of Bell Labs, says Bell realized transistors were too big for any one company to handle.

But outsiders could get at Bell's patents without paying anything in advance by taking advantage of Radio Corporation of America's cross-licensing deal in electronics with Western Electric. RCA, itself under a Justice Department investigation that culminated in filing of an antitrust suit in 1954, offered the Bell patents without requiring deposits.

By 1954, several dozen companies were turning out transistors. Some of them had taken out RCA licenses but never paid any royalties at all: They gambled on the possibility that the legal action would result in freeing the patents. And this was how it turned out. In 1958, RCA signed a consent decree ending the suit and releasing nearly all its existing patents royalty-free; shortly before it did this, it forgave all back royalties. In 1956, two years earlier, AT&T had signed a decree leaving Western Electric in the family but freeing the Bell patents up to then to one and all.

Bell Labs now has an open licensing policy for all patents awarded since the 1956 decree. Each license is negotiated individually. If the licensee is a manufacturer only, royalties are relatively high. But if it also does research and is a fertile source of new knowledge, royalties are scaled low or even waived in return for cross-licensing.

The result of this policy is that, although Bell's patents are open to the public, the Labs are able to stay pretty well at the top in semiconductor technology. Just about everybody has to come to Bell Labs for the industry's basic recipes, and cross-licensing gives Bell access to the others' findings. There are few technical secrets that cannot be discovered, either by licensing or by raiding a competitor's staff.

The availability of patents wasn't the only factor encouraging an industry free-for-all. The Defense Department helped, too, by never putting a high security classification on semiconductor devices. (Some scientists are convinced that the Pentagon never really understood the transistor's implications.)

Better ways to produce

The *D* in R&D has been important in the semiconductor industry's swift rise. At one time in the industry's early years, Zenith Radio Corporation ran big newspaper advertisements to apologize for its defective hearing aids— and blamed the defects on the transistors it was obtaining from suppliers. The trouble stemmed from water vapor that seeped into the devices and contaminated them.

The problem was remedied by improving the seal on transistors' metal cases, but it was typical of the production woes that afflicted the industry in its toddling stage. Although slightly more than one million transistors, valued at $4.8 million, were manufactured in 1954, no one had yet found a really satisfactory way to make them.

In producing transistors, there are anywhere from six to sixty different factors, or parameters, that must be taken into account. These include power-handling capacity, operating voltage, amplifying characteristics, maximum operating frequency, failure rate, and many others. They determine what kind of transistor the product will be, and each parameter must meet rigid tests.

Most of the parameters are determined by the characteristics of the transistor's base layer, its most critical area. A transistor can be pictured as a sandwich in which the base layer—often less than a thousandth of an inch thick—is the meat. In general, the thinner the base layer, the higher the operating frequency. The larger the base area, the more power the unit can handle. But as the base layer gets larger and thinner, it becomes harder and harder to make.

In 1955, there were two principal techniques for producing this transistor sandwich. The simplest and still most common method is to alloy dots of impurity elements on opposite sides of a thin slice of germanium or silicon. The time and temperature of baking in the alloy process control the depth to which the impurities penetrate and so control the base thickness.

The other way is to grow a junction in a single crystal. By adding impurities to the melt as the crystal is slowly withdrawn, impurity layers are placed across the diameter of the crystal. The crystal can then be cut into thousands of small bars, each spanning the impurity layers, and each bar can become a transistor merely by the attachment of wires to the ends and to the base.

Unhappily, neither the alloy- nor grown-junction technique yields a uniform product. At the end of a run, the transistors must be sorted by complex electronic testing into as many as a dozen or more categories. Until this testing, it is impossible to assess the device's character or how much it is worth. High-frequency units command the highest prices, and sometimes nearly an entire batch is salable. But not always. With results so unpredictable, it is difficult to balance production against demand.

The industry has tried almost every conceivable trick

to control these variables. Despite some significant progress, there is general agreement that both alloy- and grown-junction processes are close to their optimums. It took another break-through to make the next improvement possible.

That break-through came in 1955, when Bell Labs came up with the diffusion method. It produced an impurity layer on wafers of single-crystal germanium or silicon by heating the material in an atmosphere containing gaseous impurities. This diffused the impurities into the surface. Before it was possible to use this method, though, Bell's scientists had to identify and control other impurities that interfered with the material's talents as semiconductors when heated to diffusion temperatures. Those impurities were deadly in such small amounts that no method of analysis could detect them. During the long search, Bell nicknamed the villains Deathnium and Thermium; these, after four years, turned out to be copper in germanium and gold in silicon.

To the researchers' delight, the diffusion method made it possible to control the thickness of the base layer to within less than a millionth of an inch simply by adjusting the time and temperature of heating. With this technique, the base layer could cover a wide area and still be produced close to specifications. Thickness could be controlled more than ten times better than with the alloy- or grown-junction methods.

The most promising type of diffused-base transistor got its name from its appearance: it resembles the geologic formation known as a mesa. An etching process during production leaves little mounds that look, under a microscope, something like the flattened hills of the Western deserts. The name caught on.

The first diffused-base transistor was manufactured by Western Electric. The first to be generally marketed was a high-frequency germanium device introduced by Texas Instruments in the spring of 1956. The first silicon transistor of the new sort came from Fairchild Semiconductor Corporation, now a subsidiary wholly owned by Fairchild Camera and Instrument Corporation, which, largely on this one product, built sales from less than half a million dollars in 1958 to about seven million dollars in 1959.

The mesa transistor has yet to hit the industry with full impact. But it soon will. Almost every transitor maker is rushing to produce the devices. More than twenty companies will include facilities to turn them out in new plants under construction or in advanced planning. (Almost everything one writes about the semiconductor industry is a little out of date as soon as one writes it.)

The mesa type has many beauties. First, of course, there is the way the thickness of the critical base layer can be tailored. Manufacturers can vary its characteristics according to special needs, even on relatively short production runs—"just by changing the bake in this little oven, it comes out right on the nose," as a Motorola engineer describes his company's mesa line. The mesa works in the very high-frequency range—in hundreds of megacycles per second, compared to the 10 megacycles at which the best mass-produced alloy units function. It's rugged, and it's good at dissipating heat. Finally, it's cheaper to produce.

Despite the mesa's promise, a low-cost, high-yield production line already in operation for alloy- or grown-junction transistors will probably return profits for many years. But the mesa is likely to take over in most new products. "It's the first process," says J. A. Morton, vice-president of Bell Labs, "that has ever lasted four years without a better technique turning up."

Bigger yields

Morton's confidence is easy to understand from some of the mesa's yield records—the percentage of units starting out in production that end up salable. Some companies are turning out high-performance mesa transistors to rigid specifications, with yields of more than 60 per cent, and many predict yields of more than 90 per cent when the bugs are out of production lines. Such a showing in high-frequency transistors would have been utterly impossible with previous production methods.

Production yields have always been one of the semi-conductor industry's most jealously guarded secrets. Yields are the most influential of all factors affecting prices. They are also inseparable from the question of whether or not production should be mechanized—a lively issue in the industry today.

Turning out a transistor with most present techniques

takes much delicate handwork of a sort to which women seem best adapted. Currently, more than 80 per cent of the industry's 40,000 employees are women.

When technology changes as fast as it does in semiconductors, it's much cheaper to retrain workers than to rebuild expensive automatic machinery. This is a potent argument against extensive mechanizing. But human hands can't always be counted on to keep products uniform enough. Most companies think the mechanization, with its improved control over variables, is the best route to high yields. Many transistor makers have plunged into automation, praying that the equipment can be written off before the product becomes obsolete.

With alloy transistors, yields now range from about 50 per cent to a little more than 90 per cent. A typical batch might test out this way: 20 per cent high-frequency, high-performance units selling at $6 or more each; 20 per cent medium high-frequency units bringing $1.50 to $2 apiece; 40 per cent entertainment-quality transistors salable for 45 cents to $1.50; and 20 per cent expensive junk.

The entertainment-quality devices, for radios, television sets, hearing aids, and such, score the highest yields. Their tolerances are broad, and they have been longest in production. Since volume runs high, manufacturing of these units has been almost completely automated by some companies.

Texas Instruments has recently installed a desk-size, merry-go-round machine that picks up alloyed chips of semiconductor material, welds on the tiny leads, attaches the leads to wires, etches and washes the assembly, and passes it on to a bake oven. Then it is automatically capped and graded. Running unattended most of the time, the line does well indeed on yields, with much of the output in the 50-cent class for the entertainment market.

By contrast, another manufacturer crows about 90 per cent–plus yields from large-volume hand production of a germanium-alloy transistor of very broad tolerance. "We're making a fabulous profit," exults the product manager, "and I wouldn't touch the line now.... There is only 6 cents' worth of labor in the device; so suppose I could take out 4 cents by automating—and I'm not at all sure that's possible. Would it be worth a $10,000 gamble on equipment? If my yield slipped even 2 per cent, I couldn't possibly pay for the machinery."

But Philco, for one, has almost completely mechanized its production of high-speed microalloyed switching transistors for computers, with lines turning out several hundred units an hour and only eight employees per line. Some of Philco's competitors contend that this production rate is too slow to justify the several hundred thousand dollars invested in each line. It is more general for semiconductor makers to mechanize gradually, with emphasis on operations that seem least likely to change, such as encapsulation and testing. Texas Instruments has even put two of its own testing machines on the open market, though without spectacular sales results so far.

Plummeting prices

As mechanization and other methods improve yields, prices will plummet. Dramatic price cuts have been part of the industry's way of life almost since birth. It doesn't look that way from the average price paid for a transistor, which increased from $2.41 in 1958 to about $2.50 in 1959. But that was a statistical oddity: Luckily for the industry, the explosive growth in sales of relatively expensive units offset plunges in prices of other lines. An example of those plunges comes from a computer maker. In mid-1958, it paid $3.50 for a switching transistor to go into its high-speed printer. Early in 1959, the price dropped to $2.50 and then continued in a steady decline. In the spring of 1960, its price was $1.70. For a high-speed switching transistor with much tighter specifications, the same manufacturer started out paying $40. The bill in early 1960 was $12.50, and the company expected it to fall to $5 before long.

Even more spectacular is the price history of a Philco high-performance switching transistor. Introduced in sample lots at $100 each in 1956, it came on the market in May, 1957, at $60. By September of the same year, it was down to $19, and in February of 1960 it could be had in lots of 1,000 for $6.75 apiece. There are two reasons for the skid: competition and increased yields.

These factors will continue to push prices down. A hint of the future pattern of prices comes from a prediction of manufacturing costs by A. E. Anderson, manager of Western Electric's largest transistor plant. Anderson forecasts that diffused-base transistors of the mesa type will cost about half as much to produce as alloy transistors, now the most common and least costly type. Anderson based his estimates on full mechanization of production. But he did not take into account possible break-throughs that might eliminate the metal case in which transistors are sealed. This case often costs as much to make as the transistor itself. There are two ways to do away with the case, both developed at Bell Labs: One method protects the transistor by building up a silicon oxide coating; the other, by using a low-melting-point glass.

Using the oxide process to eliminate the case, Pacific Semiconductors is already selling diodes, and it has distributed experimental mesa transistors the size of a pinhead. Motorola is testing many devices with a glass surface. Many other companies are hard at work on both techniques. If the transistor case and its high added cost can be entirely eliminated, prices can be pushed down even further.

It is nothing new, of course, for a new product to bring a high price at first and a low one later. The first ball-point pens, for instance, cost the customer $15; now you can buy a ball-point, and a better one at that, for a quarter. In just the same way, junction transistors dropped from $100 to about 50 cents.

By taking the profits from the early high prices and repeatedly plowing them back into research and expansion, the semiconductor industry has been able to bring out a flood of new products, each commanding a handsome price to begin with. (This is the pattern in the drug industry as well.) Only one of the semiconductor industry's products has so far become obsolete—the point-contact transistor. Even these are still turned out at the rate of about forty thousand a year by Western Electric for use in automatic long-distance dial systems.

It is by no means certain, however, that the semiconductor industry can continue this pricing pattern indefinitely. It is nagged by some vexing questions: How fast and how far can it reduce prices without endangering its ability to maintain a flow of profitable new products? When will it start behaving like a normal industry and standardize products? If it does standardize, will price competition become so frightful that no one can make a decent profit?

The fight for position

As the industry matures, it must grapple with questions such as these, and millions of dollars ride on finding the right answers. So far, the answer has generally been research and more research to keep technologically ahead. Practically every manufacturer claims it's at the top in percentage of the sales dollar reinvested in research and plant.

In most cases, though, it's difficult to tell just how much a semiconductor maker takes in and plows back; most of them are divisions of larger corporations, and the figures are buried inside the company's over-all statistics. But a fairly clear picture of the industry's inner workings emerges from a look at the independents that do all or most of their business in semiconductors—such as Texas Instruments.

Texas Instruments leads the industry in sales, and in technology it is considered second only to Bell. In 1959, it scored net sales of $193 million, about half attributable to its broad product line of semiconductors, which includes silicon and germanium transistors of all types, silicon diodes and rectifiers, and silicon-controlled rectifiers. Compare this with its 1947 sales of less than $5 million, almost all of it from performing geophysical services, the business in which the company started. From 1953 to 1959, stockholders' equity in TI multiplied better than eight times— to $56.7 million—and the stock has been a speculators' favorite, although it has never paid a dividend. It whooshed from about $5 a share in 1952 to a 1959 high of $191. After-tax earnings in 1959 were more than 7 per cent of sales.

Most of TI's growing has been done on self-generated capital, thanks to the semiconductor-components division, undoubtedly the company's most profitable operation. The company has won its eminence by astute assessment of new products and canny timing. Its broad technological skills have made it first with many semiconductor devices.

TI's prowess began to show up in 1954. The company was first to turn out silicon transistors that would operate at temperatures of about 100 degrees C or 212 F. and the competition didn't catch up for a year and a half. TI was also first to demonstrate how to build a semiconductor market. By cutting prices drastically on a line of germanium transistors and providing circuit design and a lot of persuasion, TI promoted the little Regency portable transistor radio, made by Industrial Development Engineering Associates, Inc., of Indianapolis. The set caught on, and TI was first to profit from transistors in the mass market—though, according to industry gossip, it sank about $2 million into the project first. Latecomers in the transistor radio market had to be satisfied with a slower return.

To score these firsts, TI has spent lavishly for research and development—$30 million in 1959, half from its own funds and the other half contributed by the Federal government for specific projects. All in all, 1,400 of the semiconductor-components division's 6,000 employees devote full time to research, product development, engineering support, and patents.

TI's central research staff—including 160 degree-holding engineers, mathematicians, chemists, metallurgists, and physicists—leans heavily toward work in semiconductor materials. Gordon Teal, a Bell Labs alumnus who is research director, describes the staff's activity as "basic, but not pure" research—meaning that he limits projects "to areas of some relevance to the future of TI."

The company also has a unique production-engineering group numbering nearly five hundred, which builds almost all TI's production equipment. "When you have to make something that nobody else ever made," says

Frederick Stote, mechanization manager, "you can't very well go out and buy equipment to do it."

Obviously, only an exceptional combination of growth and profitable products can support such a concentration of employees on R&D. So far, TI has had the right combination, and there is no sign yet that it might settle down to nothing but standardized products. But the company is trying to protect itself from any future thinning of profit margins by integrating vertically and horizontally. The vertical movement is into raw materials on one hand, instruments and other electronic devices using semiconductor products on the other. It has a deal with International Business Machines to share in comprehensive research on computer components; in return, IBM will buy a substantial percentage of TI transistors for its data-processing equipment—a market that is nowhere near satiation.

Texas Instruments is also diversifying horizontally into other electronic components, such as silicon resistors and tantalum capacitors. And it is ardently committed to solid-state circuits; it is the only company so far to offer solid-state-function devices in quantities large enough to be commercial.

For the semiconductor industry as a whole, what lies ahead? The business is obviously still in ferment. When will the brew stabilize?

The traditional leaders in the electronics industry are scrambling like mad to overtake the successful independents in semiconductors. Some, such as Westinghouse, which has concentrated on high-power devices, have tended to play a waiting game until either the market stabilizes or their scientists come up with something unique. Others have rushed into the business headlong. Meantime, other established companies have diversified into semiconductors; an example is Hughes Aircraft Co., whose semiconductor division quickly took the lead in diode manufacturing and sale. Makers of electronic products joined the fun, too, as a step toward vertical integration.

This turbulent American industry faces new imponderables, especially the sudden upsurge of foreign competition and the results of still further probing into the many areas still unexplored, which could bring fresh revolutions in materials, new devices, more improvement of existing products, and wide new markets.

The peril overseas

Rivalry from abroad is relatively new to American semiconductor makers. But it is already stiff—and it will get worse. Japan is currently the most potent competitor. Imports of Japanese transistors, mostly of entertainment-quality prices of 50 cents, rocketed from 11,000 units worth $7,000 in 1958 to 1.8 million units valued at $1.1 million in the first nine months of 1959. That is still far short of a significant share of the United States market, but the growth is explosive. And United States customers bought $37.5 million worth of Japanese radio receivers, the majority of them transistor sets, in the first nine months of 1959—twice as many as in all of 1958. Texas Instruments, for one, claims that its 50-cent entertainment-grade transistors can meet this competition from the Orient. But it fears that the imports of transistor radios might cut into United States radio production—and thus slice the demand for United States transistors.

A growing semiconductor industry in Europe is also a threat. It has been perhaps a year or so behind the United States in know-how, but it is catching up fast. The leader at present is probably Philips of Eindhoven; among its exploits is an unusual alloy-diffusion process employed to make a low-priced, high-frequency transistor. This device is being manufactured in the United States through a Philips subsidiary, Amperex Electronic Corporation of Hicksville, New York.

American and foreign semiconductor companies have a variety of deals to exchange technical and financial help. General Electric, for example, is related to two Japanese electronics outfits—it owns 7 per cent of Toshiba and has given some of its licenses to Hitachi. Westinghouse has licensed Mitsubishi to make its rectifiers. Many United States companies have set up foreign subsidiaries and have built plants abroad.

In reverse arrangements, Westinghouse holds United States rights to a process for producing ultra-pure silicon developed by Siemens & Halske, a German concern. Japan's Sony Corporation has given both GE and RCA a good deal of aid in developing the tunnel, or Esaki, diode, named for its inventor, Leo Esaki. GE was one of the first to turn out tunnel diodes in quantity. It has announced development of a new tunnel diode, made of gallium arsenide, that may push operating frequencies as high as 4,000 megacycles per second. The gallium arsenide in this new tunnel diode is one of the semiconductor materials that hold promise for the future. It and other elements such as bismuth telluride may prove very useful in some jobs, particularly at high temperatures and frequencies. Other elements under study, including tungsten carbide and diamond, won't be competitive without more breakthroughs in metallurgy. Researchers are working feverishly to perfect new materials, partly because of a hope that they will open new uses for semiconductors. For a long time, though, germanium and silicon will undoubtedly hang on to their dominance.

Quest for new materials

In materials, the prospect that gives the industry most pause is that technology might make it possible for today's material suppliers also to become competitive producers. Such a shift could conceivably shake the entire business. Currently, some semiconductor materials come from outside suppliers, some from captive sources. Almost all germanium oxide is purchased from companies outside the industry, but Sylvania produces its own.

A change in supplier-producer relationships might come through development of new thin-film techniques to make semiconductor crystals. One major supplier, Merck & Co., diligently at work in this area, has already produced single crystals of silicon with multiple junctions by a vapor-deposition method. Perfection of this technique would mean that the material would only have to be sliced into small dice before it could be processed into transistors. It would take only one more step for the transistor maker to produce complete devices. The method holds great promise for growing complex circuits right in the crystal.

This possibility isn't too farfetched. There is some feeling that both the making and processing of superpure materials belong to the chemical industry. But many semiconductor firms are moving to protect themselves, by contracting with material suppliers or developing captive sources of materials of their own.

In the development of devices using these materials, semiconductor companies are following two paths: expanding the versatility of existing products such as transistors and designing wholly new devices for new jobs.

New uses, new devices

It used to be that transistors were best for low-power, low-frequency chores, such as in a portable radio, but impractical at high power and frequency, as in a VHF radio transmitter. But transistors and other semiconductor devices are becoming more and more proficient. Just about the only place where they show no signs of competing with tubes is in extremely high-power uses, such as commercial radio transmitters and UHF microwave and radar transmitters.

As prices of powerful, high-frequency devices drop, some

rich markets will open. When transistors come into the price range of present television-set tubes, there will almost certainly be a mass shift away from tubes. Some predict the switch will begin this year. Automobile radios will soon be completely transistorized.

Of the industry's new devices, the most exciting is the Esaki diode, which amplifies a current by making use of an obscure phenomenon known as negative resistance. Researchers forecast a brilliant future for the Esaki diode in computers and as a high-frequency oscillator. A GE model of gallium arsenide has generated frequencies of 4 billion or 5 billion cycles per second—frequencies high enough to make it possible to build computers with the logical capacity of the human brain. Tokyo University scientists are working on just such a computer. The Esaki diode may also shine as a high-frequency amplifier in FM radio and television sets, where it would be used in conjunction with transistors.

Probably the most important of all developments is the work in circuit-function packages—wrapping the entire works of something like a radio into one tiny, utterly dependable chunk. There are three simultaneous approaches to this project:

• The Army Signal Corps microminiature module, for which RCA holds the prime contract. Well along toward volume production, this involves putting transistor elements, resistors, and such on tiny ceramic squares, which are then stacked in a wire cage. The final unit is potted in plastic.

• A second technique, high in favor at Bell Labs: Whole circuits are placed on one ceramic disk, which is then encapsulated. This way, several transistors can be used without separate capsules.

• The solid-circuit-function package, known as molectronics, demonstrated by Texas Instruments and Westinghouse and under development in many other laboratories. The semiconductor crystal is used as resistor, transistor, and capacitor—even under a microscope, the elements can't be separated. By eliminating most interconnections, this method may well bring a huge improvement in reliability. Texas Instruments has shown off a computer counter that normally would be as big as a shoe box, with more than eighty different elements. Using solid-state circuits, it has only eleven elements and is no bigger than a lead pencil's rubber eraser. Westinghouse has devised a phonograph amplifier the size of a single transistor.

Many engineers still doubt that circuit-function packages will ever be economically practical. But most in the industry disagree. A Texas Instruments engineer describes how his company can use a single crystal of silicon for a device that would have formerly been made up of more than a dozen components costing $100 in all. "It's not only more reliable," he says, "but eventually it will be considerably cheaper."

That single silicon crystal is no bigger than a match head, but it contains the guts of a two-tube radio.

The industry won't stop at swallowing up the vacuum tube. If no one else makes products containing circuit-function devices, it may make them itself. One executive who refused to be identified "because I always make a fool of myself by underestimating," predicts: "The industry will pass the billion-dollar level in two years with just the devices it now has in production. Add circuit functions, and you can double that figure." And Bell's Morton concludes: "There's not a shred of doubt in my mind that electronics will soon be the largest industry in the United States, thanks largely to solid-state devices."

But the semiconductor industry's greatest contribution to national economic growth will not come directly from its own growth—but from its contribution to the entire industrial process. It's one of the potent forces behind that continuously rising productivity curve that economists can only imperfectly measure, and understand still less.

Scarcity of brains

To make its maximum contribution to national economic growth, however, the semiconductor industry must solve its greatest single problem—a problem that affects all industries in some degree during the research revolution. That problem is the finding of enough brains to go around. There's no such animal as a semiconductor engineer, as such—companies have had to make their own from chemists, physicists, electronic engineers, and other specialists. Even then, once a man has established his expertise, there is no guarantee that he won't succumb to attractive offers from competitors.

Scientists with a name in the field get several calls a

month at home from recruiters. As salaries rise, so do a company's fixed costs. "You can't get anyone today," one division manager complains, "unless you can offer him a stock option."

A canny job jumper can sometimes double and redouble his salary before employers discover he really wasn't worth the original amount. But, fortunately, most of the industry's brains are more serious about their calling.

Another personnel problem is the likelihood that a top-notch semiconductor man will be hoisted out of the laboratory and into a top executive's armchair; but there are real managerial shortages, too. In such a technical industry, the top brass practically has to run heavily to scientists. This thins the research ranks.

Some of the men at the top are among today's most glamorous business successes. Starting with outstanding scientific skills and practically no capital, they are now worth millions. A good many of the industry's experts got their training and grew up at Bell Labs—which, besides supplying semiconductor makers with a cookbook, provided many of the best chefs. Whatever the company, though, it is likely at some time to have lost key people— occasionally in batches. For instance, men from Hughes's semiconductor division formed Pacific Semiconductors, Inc., a division of Thompson Ramo Wooldridge. An exodus from Radio Receptor Corporation led to creation of General Transistor Corporation. Alumni of General, in turn, split off into Industro Transistor Corporation and Silicon Transistor Corporation. Transitron (founded by a young Harvard-trained physicist, David Bakalar, and his big brother Leo) lost a group that established Solid State Products, Inc., which then beat Transitron to market with a silicon-controlled rectifier, a device pioneered by General Electric.

These are exciting days for smart, well-trained, energetic people.

5

The General Shortage of Brain Power

Americans, it is said, are becoming a race of timid, conformist, nonentities—other-directed organization men, wearing their gray-flannel suits to their corporate crystal palaces, group-thinking the group thoughts imposed upon them by both hidden and public persuaders.

And opposition to this trend has virtually become a Movement: All about us we hear journalists, sociologists, preachers, advertising men, political candidates, subur-

banites, exurbanites, movers back to the city and those
who had never left the city, our friends—even ourselves—
bewailing and berating this brain-washed, conformist society.

But a hesitant question suggests itself: If there are so
many beraters of conformity, is there not some danger that
we will soon run into a shortage of conformists? It reminds
one a bit of the 1920s, when everyone joined in a mass
attack on American society as cramped, crabbed, blue-
stockinged, Babbitty, inhibited—though that period has
in fact gone down in the history books as the Roaring
Twenties, the golden age of the pursuit of life, liberty, and
happiness, however nutty. Surely the cultural heroes of the
twenties were Freud, Mencken, Sinclair Lewis, Scott Fitz-
gerald, if not Texas Guinan and Legs Diamond. Against
them, Volstead, Calvin Coolidge—and Babbitt—didn't
stand a chance; they were, as Arnold Toynbee would say,
fossils.

Our easy, almost unconscious acceptance today of a wider
degree of freedom in personal conduct and literary and
artistic taste suggests the extent of the victory of the 1920s
over traditional American puritanism—and how lasting
and widening a victory it has proved to be.

And I wonder whether the current massive assault on
conformity may not, somewhat similarly, be a manifesta-
tion of a major current in American thought that will
prove to establish the really significant tone of our new
epoch more conclusively than do the instances of con-

formity which are under such widespread and furious attack.

The attack of the 1920s was, after all, also against conformity—but conformity to the morals and manners of the American small town, as the nation went urban. The new assault on conformity, on the other hand, is focused essentially on the restrictive, inhibiting morals and manners of the large business corporation. Where once it was the small town that was said to cramp the American individual, cheapen his life, so today it is the large corporation, the dominant institution in American life, which casts over all its servants a gray-flannel pallor, which is said to be spreading to all other institutions and their servants —to the colleges and universities, the press, the research foundations, the government, the political parties—so that finally all the variegated colors of free and individual Americans will be washed away.

But is it true? Is it really true? Is the intellectual crowd right? Does the king really wear gray-flannel clothes? Do the "types" really exist? I find myself wondering, like Lillian McCall,[1] "Who are the disembodied abstractions —those 'fantastic beings' that Tocqueville warned us would make us regret the world of reality—haunting the brains of social scientists and 'social critics'?" Where, she asks, are we to find the Conformist, the Market Place Personality, the Unproductively Oriented, the Other Directed —"to say nothing of the Inner Confused crawling in and

[1] *Commentary,* June, 1957.

out of the various pigeonholes in search of 'the real self' ... ," or the Part-time Lady, the Mass-produced Eccentric, and the Upper Bohemian. "The less people are understood," says Mrs. McCall, "the more they are classified."

And I wonder whether, in this specific attack on the individual-freedom-destroying nature of the modern corporation, our social critics are not simply persisting in one of the most familiar themes in social criticism throughout the past two centuries: the attack on the industrial system, on modern science and technology.

Romanticism

From the industrial revolution of the eighteenth century to this day, poets like Schiller, Wordsworth, and Auden,[2]

> ... the new barbarian is no uncouth
> Desert-dweller; he does not emerge
> From fir forests: factories bred him;
> Corporate companies, college towns
> Mothered his mind. ...

novelists like Dickens, Tolstoi, and Faulkner, philosophers and political thinkers like Adam Müller, Fichte, Spengler, Kierkegaard, and a host of other artists from Henry David Thoreau to D. H. Lawrence—have been denouncing the industrial system as the annihilator of human values.[3]

[2] W. H. Auden, *The Age of Anxiety*, Random House, New York, 1946.

[3] See the novels of C. P. Snow, which describe the basic cleavage of Western culture into two cultures—one scientific and one literary. But, curiously enough, many scientists, in their more general social thinking, tend to

Over the years, however, the specific charges on the bill of indictment against the industrial system have changed. In the early years of the industrial revolution, it was condemned for throwing families off the land, for herding them into wretched factories and factory towns, for destroying their traditional culture, for debasing men and women into moving parts of the industrial machine, and even for impoverishing them. You find this in Karl Marx; you also find it in the whole romantic movement of the nineteenth century which Nietzsche called "... the counterstroke to the eighteenth century: a sort of accumulated longing for the grand style of exaltation (as a matter of fact, largely mingled with mummery and self-deception: the desire was to represent strong nature and strong passion)."

Much later, with the coming of the assembly line, the system was still being condemned for turning people into pitiful automatons (like Charlie Chaplin's factory worker in *Modern Times*) who can scarcely shake off the rhythm of the machine even after the workers leave the factory; and the system was damned, even more harshly, for demoralizing the people by mass unemployment, just so industry could always draw upon what Marx called "the reserve army of the unemployed" and so keep wages at the lowest possible level.

---

fall into the "literary" category in their hostility to modern industrialism, to "business" and all its works. Indeed, it may be that the best way of categorizing the cultural split might be between the literary culture and the business culture. But, obviously, no simple two-way split will adequately describe the conflicts within our culture.

Now, long after the Great Depression, after many years of economic growth and something close to full employment, the industrial system is being denounced for producing a new breed of submissive, faceless men—for choking men with affluence—and possibly for creating an automatic production system that will end by making people obsolete.

Industrialism and freedom

Yet, as so often in the past, anxieties aroused by the industrial system appear to be concealing the system's tremendous power, not to dehumanize people, but to free men for the use of their highest faculties.

In a sense there is nothing new about this. As Lee DuBridge has said, "It was knowledge of nature's laws that abolished the fear of demons; it was the steam engine that ended slavery; it was the power machines that gave men freedom from hunger-driven toil, and thus made all other freedoms possible." Of course, most of the world is still struggling to attain those human freedoms enjoyed in the highly industrialized countries. It is mostly just Western sentimentalists who can detect much serenity or joy in the hunger-haunted, disease-ridden, preindustrial countries.

Yet, even the most highly developed industrial nations may have only begun to experience the opportunities for expanding the range of human freedom that industrialism offers.

Technological development, as it grows more complex, affects a people in two fundamental ways:

• It puts a high premium on educated human intelligence, creates enormous demands for people capable of using their intelligence. Far from imposing intellectual conformity, it calls urgently for men who can reason objectively, challenge dogmas or existing customs, discover new ideas.

• By increasing production faster than population growth, it solves the problem of satisfying man's physical needs. As a result, it is bringing greater potentialities for improvement of human talents—for their employment both at work and after work—and for their extension to a broader share of the entire population than ever before. Past societies solved the problem of providing amply for the physical and intellectual requirements of a small elite group by making slaves or serfs or other sorts of wretches out of practically everybody else; the modern industrial system is the first which promises to extend such privileges to everybody.

This double effect of the modern industrial system—which puts human intelligence on the highest pedestal—is not some vague future possibility, wishful thinker's daydream. It has already struck the American society with a force that few comprehend; and it cannot be checked. It's rapidly multiplying the urgent need for highly educated, creatively intelligent men—and multiplying it so fast that the educational processes can't keep up.

Even if Americans were content to rest on their present attainments, it might be national suicide—in a period of competitive coexistence and cold war—to stay at that level. The real foundation for the nation's strength is human knowledge. The need for more people with knowledge has already become evident in every area of American life.

Where the need is

There is hardly anyone today who has not encountered some aspect of this spreading need for educated talent. But these aspects are so varied that few have realized the impact in its totality. Each area feels its own critical need:

• Business and industry—for scientists, engineers, managers, highly trained technicians.

• Government—for these, and for people skilled in international relations, languages, public administration, the social sciences.

• The Armed Forces—for highly trained officers, enlisted men, and civilians able to develop and operate a more and more complex military machine.

• And the entire society—for outstanding organizers and leaders—those who set the goals that stir others to their best efforts.

One symptom of the over-all need is the cacophony of charges that skilled engineers are wasting their time on technicians' jobs, that highly trained people are being "drained away" to other jobs—teachers into industry, engineers into management, fundamental scientists into applied research, and so on—or that companies are "hoarding" scientists and engineers and managers away from each other.

Most people assume all this is simply a phenomenon born of the economic boom and wonder if it will evaporate if the economy slips down to a slower pace. That could, of course, happen—as a short-run development. But the growing need for educated talent is founded on a more durable base than the short-run business cycle.

During and just after World War II, many experts did regard the brain-power shortage as a transitory phase; some did scholarly analyses to show that we were training too many teachers, engineers, and other white-collar intellectuals. There were fears that this might set the stage for a nasty social explosion by these educated but unusable groups—as in the prewar Fascist and Communist movements, which were often led by embittered, unemployed "intellectuals."

Such fears were groundless. The demand for educated people, far from contracting as the extreme wartime needs tapered off, actually continued to grow—through prosperity and four moderate postwar recessions. There is every indication that it will go on growing in the years ahead.

Nobody knows better than American industrialists how steeply the need for educated people has been rising. Not every industry is so dependent on brain power as the semiconductor industry, which we have examined in some detail, but virtually every industry has greatly increased its staff of college-educated people during the postwar years. For instance, the Ford Motor Co. recently said it employs approximately five times as many persons actually holding college degrees as it did ten years ago; International Nickel said three to four times as many; Air Reduction Co. said five to six times as many.

But it is not just college-educated brains that are in heavy demand and relatively short supply. The scarcity of trained supporting technicians is just as acute. Indeed, that is part of the reason for the engineering shortage: In the United States, engineers have to do technicians' work. In this country, there is just one supporting technician for every three engineers; in Europe, the ratio is three technicians for every engineer.

Upgrading the labor force

What is happening, as a result of rapid technological advance in this country, is in reality more than a brain-power shortage—if we think of brain power as scientists, engineers, and other college-degree holding specialists; more than that, we are experiencing a massive upgrading of the skills and training required of the entire United States labor force, and a shift from employment directly in the production process to other sorts of jobs. All the so-called white-collar groups—supervisors, technicians, clerical and professional people—have been growing much faster than the blue-collar (production) workers. This has been a very long-term trend. In the last fifty years, while production workers increased by 75 per cent, white-collar workers increased by 200 per cent. In 1957, we reached a historic turning point, when the white-collar group became the biggest single segment of the labor force, outnumbering the blue-collar workers for the first time. In the years ahead the white-collar class will claim a larger and larger share of the labor force, as the blue-collar groups continue to contract.

As we have been learning in recent years, these shifts are far from painless for many of the people caught in the declining sectors, such as manufacturing, mining, and agriculture. The shifts can mean fairly heavy and persistent unemployment in places like West Virginia or Michigan, for surplus coal miners or auto workers, as well as for older workers, as a group, who may find it especially hard to reeducate themselves for new jobs.

The research revolution means that this shift from brawn to brains, from production to nonproduction work, is going to continue, possibly to accelerate. The reason becomes clear when you look at the way the whole industrial system operates in its complex current version. You start with the people who create new ideas, the scientists; and they are desperately scarce. Then you need people to engineer these ideas into things or processes; and they are also in short supply. Guiding this process—assembling, organizing, and directing the people and the equipment for getting the engineered ideas into production—demands high-caliber managers, men who can see how all parts of the process can best be put together; and such managers are extremely scarce, too, as the executive recruiters and management developers will tell you.

Then you need workers. The kind who can design or make or repair the machines are in hot demand, but the ones who just work along with the machines, or are doing work that machines can take over, are not. When the goods are produced, they have to be marketed—and sales-people and advertising men are in short supply, too.

Finally, in the background of the whole process, are the people who have to educate and train all these others and do the research that helps make the work at each step more efficient. These too are scarce.

The reason for all this is that the flow of new ideas has been fast and furious. They are ideas that do make obsolete the human types who, in their functions, resemble ma-chines. But they put tremendous demands upon those who are capable of thinking and acting with the intelligence and flexibility that is the special mark of human beings.

That's the nub of it: More complicated machinery basi-cally does two things. On one side, it takes the place of slow and inefficient human abilities, such as pushing, pull-ing, lifting, walking, remembering, counting, seeing, hear-ing, measuring, cutting, stamping, hammering, spreading information. On the other hand, it stimulates enormous demands for other human faculties involving thought and imagination—valuing, judging, sensing, spotting relations between the apparently dissimilar, taking account of subtle, nonquantifiable differences, generalizing—and creating.

Today's complex machines perform the first set of functions with an astronomical increase in efficiency as compared with humans. But even the most fantastically complex mechanical monsters can exercise or simulate the second group of human faculties at only a relatively primitive level. Just to keep the two areas in balance greatly magnifies the need for the human exercise of these talents.

The process feeds on itself: The speeding up of technological development breeds a mounting need for ever faster scientific and technological growth. As everyone consumes more energy, more natural resources, the easily available supply provided by nature dwindles more sharply. We call on science and technology to supply us with the materials and energy required by a rising population bent on higher standards of life.

Specializing and generalizing

Technological and scientific progress force human knowledge and skills into greater specialization in every field. The biologist splits into the biochemist, the biophysicist, the geneticist, the embryologist, the microbiologist, and so on—the general practitioner into the cardiologist, the gynecologist, the pediatrician, and many other specializations. And so it goes in every line.

This increasing specialization, in turn, produces a counterneed—for the integrating generalist, who can master a broad area taking in many specialties, in order to combine their achievements for wider application. The specialties, indeed, become so diverse, and so ingrown in their individual areas, that this integrating generalist may turn out to be the rarest and most valuable talent of all. What is likely to be more and more needed, as specialties multiply faster than the supply of outstanding specialists, is the development of men who are highly skilled not so much in any single specialty as in scientific processes as such. Then these men can turn quickly from one research field to another, trusting the more routine gathering and storing of information to others—or to machines.

The rising demand for educated talent is one of the most crucial aspects of the complex process of economic growth. No one can say just how long this demand for educated talent will last, or how much it will increase. Apart from all the economic, military, social, political, demographic and other factors affecting the demand for brains, particular branches of science have a sort of life and growth of their own. Basic new discoveries often seem to sprout (frequently in many widely scattered laboratories) when the scientific soil is prepared for them.

The demand for educated talent is not independent of, but is rather a function of, the supply of talent. As our semiconductor case made clear, scientific and engineering break-throughs step up the demand for more scientists and engineers.

The job of getting educated people in large enough numbers and of sufficiently high quality is one of the crucial jobs facing the nation.

Supplying the brains

For the immediate future, the outlook is not particularly hopeful.

The American educational system, as all the world knows, has been under intense strain; and those strains are still increasing. The Department of Labor has estimated that, during the 1955–1965 decade, enrollment in elementary schools will increase by 8 million, a 30 per cent rise; in high schools, by 12 million, a 60 per cent rise; and in colleges, by 2 million, a 75 per cent rise.

This oncoming tide of youth will put terrific demands on the specialized talent that must be ploughed back into educating the new generation; and unless ways can be found quickly to prevent it, this pressure on the educational system will bring a deterioration in American educational standards—thus aggravating still further the shortage of high-quality graduates of our schools, colleges, and universities. The danger is already being compounded by the inability of schools and colleges to compete with industry for new college graduates.

The Ford Foundation's Fund for the Advancement of Education has made a calculation of the number of teachers that will be needed. It figures that in order to maintain present pupil-teacher ratios and to provide for replacements and expansion, United States schools (below the college level) will have to find 16 new teachers between now and 1965 for every 10 now teaching. That is equivalent to replacing all the teachers we now have and finding 60 per cent more. For colleges and universities, it will be even more difficult.

In the next ten years, the Fund for the Advancement of Education estimates American colleges will have to add between 16 and 25 professors for every 10 they now have, to maintain the present average ratio of 13 students per teacher.

To meet those needs of the schools and colleges over the next ten years, we would have to take nearly 2 million college graduates—more than half of the 3.7 million total that is expected to come out of the colleges—just to meet the need for new teachers. As things are, only about one-fifth of all college graduates are going into school or college teaching.

The effect on educational standards could be serious. Today two-fifths of American college teachers hold Ph.D. degrees—which are certainly a measure of the amount of training, if not of qualitative merit. By 1970, the Ford Foundation estimates, only one-fifth of the college teachers may be Ph.D.s. If educational methods remain about what they are and more poorly trained teachers must face much larger classes, the decay of standards could be cumulative.

In high schools the effect on standards is already even more ominous; many observers regard improvement in the high schools as the really crucial point, the key to an increase (or decrease) in the number of those able to go on to difficult scientific work in college. In the five years from 1950 to 1955, there was a sharp decline in the output of new high school teachers in important subjects: The output of teachers of mathematics declined by 51 per cent; among science teachers, the decline was 57 per cent.

As the shortage of qualified teachers mounts, more emergency teachers are hired, and more children get part-time schooling on double sessions.

Nearly everyone is willing to concede that the United States faces one of its most fundamental problems in this question of how to handle the oncoming mass of new students and how to provide them with the upgraded education that is demanded by the growing complexity of science, technology, and the whole economy. But there is still sharp disagreement among educators and laymen alike over how to go about the job.

Some—among them the heads of the Fund for the Advancement of Education—would seek ways of rapidly increasing the productivity and effectiveness of each teacher, by some method such as the use of educational television. Others fear that these "mass communications" techniques would only debase standards still further.

Some call for establishing a larger and larger number of colleges and universities to keep up with the number of students seeking entrance, and for spreading the best teachers (and best students too) more evenly throughout the nation. Others contend that the students who enroll in the very best institutions are doing the smartest thing; whatever the aggregate needs of the nation, they say, this makes for quality, and quality is the most important need of all. "I understand," says Lee DuBridge, president of California Institute of Technology, "that over half of the top men students in the country who won National Merit Scholarships—three hundred or so boys of really top ability —chose to go to about a half-dozen universities and institutes of technology, all of which are generally recognized as being the most difficult in the country to get into. Those smart boys were smart enough to know that if they were smart enough to win a scholarship, they ought to go where the smartest students are to be found."

Some complain that this is unfair to smaller and less famous institutions. But DuBridge says, "I say it is unfair to the other 50 per cent of those smart boys if they go to institutions where they will never have the competition required to develop their talents." He might even suggest, he added, that the Merit Scholarship Board should not allow any winners in the top 1 per cent to use their scholarships except at a "select few of the institutions of the country" with proved capacity to give full challenge to top talent.

There are other widely debated suggestions for strengthening education to meet the new challenge. Some see the only solution in heavy Federal outlays to improve schools, raise teachers' salaries, provide more scholarships for the able (at present, the Fund for the Advancement of Education found, more than one-half of the ablest youth does not get to college). This argument for Federal aid provokes strong opposition from others, who feel that large-scale Federal aid is bound to produce corrosive effects on the range and variety of education, and might in fact limit its freedom. In the name of liberalism, opponents of government aid to the schools remind one of the damage a Senator Joe McCarthy could have done, say, to Harvard, if Harvard had been dependent on Federal funds for its existence. Others, in the name of liberalism, are just as passionately in favor of more Federal aid to education, as a means of redressing the balance between private consumption (symbolized by the tail fins of a noncompact automobile) and public needs.

Some (such as Admiral Hyman Rickover) argue for special schools for the specially bright; others condemn this as an undemocratic and unnecessarily narrow way of trying to develop the educated talent we need.

The arguments wax hotter, but as yet they have led to little action, despite endless committee and commission inquiries. This lag in action is strong evidence that the American people have not yet taken the problem quite seriously. To be sure, that lag is nothing unusual; it commonly takes a crisis to rouse the American people to strong action. But is education an area in which a crash-program approach can make up for years of neglect? It takes a long time to build a school and college and graduate school system that can turn out a large supply of highly competent specialists (or generalists).

Anti-intellectualism

Some people think the real root of the educational crisis lies in American values—that the society has not yet come to regard education (public or private) as important as, say, sports and entertainments—that the society has not yet rid itself of the old suspicion and scorn of the long-hair, the egghead, the double-dome. But there are signs that a shift is occurring. Indeed, John W. Gardner, president of the Carnegie Corporation and a leading proponent of what he calls "the great national talent hunt," believes that the one group that seems not to have caught on to this growing appreciation for scientific and intellectual attainments are intellectuals themselves. Gardner believes that American intellectuals—like some other earlier minority groups in this country—seem not to have noticed that they have virtually left behind them their "inferior social status." The research revolution—and all the other promises and threats of this hectic century—are destroying that older image of the learned man as a sort of helpless nincompoop. Certainly, in business, industry and government respect has been growing for the skills, integrity and imagination of the really gifted scholars, researchers, thinkers. Technological change is closing the gap between business and science; as H. Gershinowitz, president of Shell Development Co. puts it, "A general appreciation of science and technology, and the real understanding of some area of their application, is now essential to a large and growing portion of top positions in business, industry, and government."

Care and feeding of intellects

Undeniably, business is coming to know and understand the intellectual much better than once it did. Not long ago I had occasion to conduct a series of interviews with about one hundred business leaders in many industries on their view of the nature and problems of scientific, professional, and "creative" manpower. Here is a composite picture of the intellectual as the executives saw him:

• He hates to be pushed around. He hates to be treated like a subordinate. His conception of his role is as the intellectual equal of anybody, regardless of rank, status, seniority.

• He has divided loyalties—not only to the company or institution that pays him, but also to his profession, to his own conscience, to scientific or abstract truth.

• He is by nature—certainly in the area of his specialty—a nonconformist. The quest for new ideas requires great skepticism about the value of old ideas, a willingness to look foolish, waste time, be a crank.

• He loves a maximum of freedom—because the quest for new ideas cannot go on except in an atmosphere of freedom.

• His feelings are easily wounded, and his concern for the inviolateness of his intellectual honor is likely to be intense. He often feels that giving in to the views of a boss represents prostitution.

• He works best when he feels that he is really his own boss, when, in other words, he feels that he has genuine responsibility for what he does, how he does it.

• He likes to feel that what he is working on is important. He hates routine work. And he often gets restless when what he conceives as the difficult or creative part of a job is over.

And, when I asked these business executives to tell me their prescription for the appropriate care and feeding of these thinkers, if they were going to do their best work, executive after executive reeled off the same kinds of prescriptions which have long been familiar in the intellectual's old haunts—the universities and the professions:

• "Provide proper recognition for the professional individual from both economic and noneconomic points of view—treat him as a truly professional person with the privileges that such persons have learned to expect."

• "Ensure that these men are not draining off their time and energy in doing a multitude of routine chores of the kind that develop around their assignment."

• "Avoid too tight organization lines, and leave people with such potential considerable leeway for the exercise of individual initiative."

• "Encourage their participation in professional societies and attendance at scientific and technical meetings."

• "See that individuals get credit and recognition for findings."

• "Make industry more and more an educational institution, equipped to train and upgrade people."

Over and over, these executives stressed the importance of providing educated people with freedom to think and to question, of encouraging them to form independent judgments and to take responsibility and initiative, and of providing individual recognition and prestige. And a number of executives made the point that these prescriptions should not be confined to the men in the laboratories

but should be extended to all parts of the organization—
for, as one Carborundum Corporation executive put it,
"All phases of the business call for creative men; crea-
tivity and initiative are not something to be bottled up
among a little group of elite intellectuals." [4]

One cannot, of course, take the word for the deed. There
are widely varying degrees in which the climate of freedom in different companies, within or beyond their research laboratories, may or may not approach the freedom
within the great universities. Obviously, as long as the
corporation's primary business is the collective aim of
making a profit and as long as the university's primary
business (leaving teaching aside) is enabling individual investigators to discover truth, differences between the corporation and the university must persist. But it would be
false and misleading to put the profit-truth division between the corporation and the university in simple black
and white terms.

Profit and truth

Indeed, in one of his most startling and insightful pas-
sages, Joseph Schumpeter held that profit-seeking capitalism was in fact the creator of truth-seeking science.[5]

---

[4] In his 1958 McKinsey Lectures at Columbia University, Crawford H.
Greenewalt, president of Du Pont, discussing ways for the corporation
to get the most out of its executives, favored fostering individual thought
and fighting against the kind of conformity that smothers identity and
fresh ideas. See Crawford H. Greenewalt, *The Uncommon Man*, McGraw-
Hill Book Company, Inc., New York, 1959.

[5] Joseph A. Schumpeter, *Capitalism, Socialism, and Democracy*, 3d ed.,
Harper & Brothers, New York, 1942, pp. 123–124.

[Capitalism] exalts the monetary unit—not itself a creation of capitalism—into a unit of account. That is to say, capitalist practice turns the unit of money into a tool of rational cost-profit calculations, of which the towering monument is double-entry bookkeeping. Without going into this, we will notice that, primarily a product of the evolution of economic rationality, the cost-profit calculus in turn reacts upon that rationality; by crystallizing and defining numerically, it powerfully propels the logic of enterprise. And thus defined and quantified for the economic sector, this type of logic or attitude or method then starts upon its conqueror's career subjugating—rationalizing—man's tools and philosophies, his medical practice, his picture of the cosmos, his outlook on life, everything in fact including his concepts of beauty and justice and his spiritual ambitions.

In this respect it is highly significant that modern mathematicoexperimental science developed, in the fifteenth, sixteenth, and seventeenth centuries, not only along with the social process usually referred to as the Rise of Capitalism, but also outside of the fortress of scholastic thought and in the face of its contemptuous hostility. In the fifteenth century mathematics was mainly concerned with questions of commercial arithmetic and the problems of the architect. The utilitarian mechanical device, invented by men of the craftsman type, stood at the source of modern physics. The rugged individualism of Galileo was the individualism of the rising capitalist class. The surgeon began to rise above the midwife and the barber. The artist who at the same time was an engineer and an entrepreneur—the type immortalized by such men as Vinci, Alberti, Cellini; even Dürer busied himself with plans for fortifications—illustrates best of all what I mean. By curs-

ing it all, scholastic professors in the Italian universities
showed more sense than we give them credit for. The
trouble was not with individual unorthodox propositions.
Any decent schoolman could be trusted to twist his texts
so as to fit the Copernican system. But those professors
quite rightly sensed the spirit behind such exploits—the
spirit of rationalist individualism, the spirit generated by
rising capitalism.

Rather than turning on the abstract—and false—issue
of profit versus truth, the major difference between the
corporation and the university would appear to turn on
organizational lines. The corporation is a massive organization where individual wills must to a greater extent
be coerced and harmonized to serve a common purpose—
to achieve certain production, sales, profit objectives, while
the university (despite, in some areas, a growing resemblance to corporate enterprise) remains basically a collection of unrelated individuals or small groups of scholars
who may be at war with each other, or even against the
university administration itself, and still be serving mankind's ultimate objectives—whatever this may or may not
do to a particular university president's fund-raising drive
or some dean's ability to attract students. The university
should not pretend to be a business corporation; a business corporation should not pretend to be a university.
Each serves society best in pursuing its own legitimate
objectives.

But the problem of individual freedom within the corporation (as it is within the United States Army, the State

Department, the AFL-CIO, or any other large organization) is one of defining the rules and limits of individual freedom; indeed, this is the problem of society itself.

Individual freedom was easy to attain in the days when most people were frontiersmen or small farmers; that was why Jefferson wanted America to stay a nation of small farmers. The growth of large organizations, as industrialism advanced, meant that, within the framework of a democratic and individualistic society, there was very little freedom in fact for workers on the job (sometimes off the job, as in company towns). Individualism of the old frontier type survived—for the boss; he had plenty of it —his employees precious little.

That situation has been changing—first under the impact of trade-union organization of the mass-production industries, which did much to define the rules and limits of managerial control over the individual, and, more recently, under the impact of what (for want of a better name) we have been calling the research revolution, and of its result, the brain-power shortage. And it is happening, not because today's top executives have become gentler, more altruistic, or perhaps more timid than were their fathers or grandfathers, but because widening the area of individual freedom and initiative within the corporation makes practical sense, serves the profit-making objective.

Certainly the wisest of corporation executives are coming to recognize that a greater measure of individual freedom, within the corporation's walls, is essential to both short-term and long-term corporate goals. The corporation, so bitterly denounced today as the very Kremlin of enforced conformity, appears to be in process of becoming an institution where more and more individuals are being encouraged to think and speak out and say no and use their imaginations. The great and growing need for creative people—and the growing recognition that they are people who can serve both the corporation and their own private and professional consciences—seems to be spreading beyond the laboratories. This may, in time, spell the demise of the corporate "true believers," cynical hacks, yes men, and time servers. Thanks to the research revolution, creative man may in the end triumph over organization man.

6

Can We Get Balanced Growth?

We have defined growth as a long-run phenomenon. But—to quote Keynes's most famous dictum—in the long run we are all dead. Long-run growth without short-run stability isn't worth much; indeed, without stability, we might all be dead in the *short* run. Problems of revolution, war, and economic stability are intertwined. Certainly the Great Depression grew out of our failure to deal with the economic consequences of World War I, and the author of World War II, Adolf Hitler, emerged like a slimy salamander from the ashes of the Great Depression.

Today, a failure to achieve both growth and stability would yield even more tragic consequences for America and the free world.

Why growth is unstable

The problems of growth and stability are also intertwined—so complexly that economists are only beginning to understand their relations. The quest for that understanding has come to center upon the investment process in a capitalist economy.

And if autonomous investment—the kind that results from cultural forces, of which the most important is human brain power, as we have been trying to show—is the chief cause of long-term economic growth, then the other category of investment, induced investment, has a different role.

Induced investment—generated by forces within the economic system and representing a response to changes in the demand for existing products—is the prime cause of short-term instability. Upswings in induced investment produce booms—and, commonly, some degree of inflation. Downswings in induced investment produce recession, unemployment, and, in the past, deflation, but more recently stable prices or just a slower rate of creeping inflation.

To be sure, if a fall in induced investment were great enough to drag down national income for a lengthy period, and to damage public and business confidence, it might have a more disastrous effect. It might contract the resources, human and financial, that otherwise would have gone into autonomous investment, or into the scientific and technological work that underlies autonomous investment.

If a depression, for example, caused industries to slash their research programs and was deep enough to starve colleges and universities both for funds and for students, the economic loss to the nation might be long-lived. The "might" is a necessary qualification, however, for it is not quite clear that even the Great Depression of the 1930s seriously retarded the long-term growth of the United States economy. It probably did hold things back to some extent—but it is hard to find the evidence for that in the long-term growth statistics which we presented in Chapter 2.

On the other hand, it is possible that relatively moderate dips in investment, which result in brief and moderate recessions, actually stimulate long-term growth. The reason is that recessions force business to step up its efficiency and encourage it to go in for innovations, either to cut costs or to create new markets. To take just one example, Warner Bros. Pictures did not launch the talking movie because it was overloaded with cash but because it was in desperate financial straits.

Of course, every innovation does not automatically give a company an antidote for sinking sales of existing products. Cinerama, Smell-O-Vision, and AromaRama do not appear to be capable of producing growing audiences for movie houses today—though there is some hint that good stories may.

Though induced investment has its own role, in the real world it's not so easy to disentangle induced from autonomous investment. When a company needs extra capacity because its sales are increasing, it does not try to build a plant exactly like the last one (or the first one) that it built. It puts up the most efficient and modern plant it can get together, throwing in all the technological advances that have come along in the meantime.

So the question is this: In the decision to build the new plant, how big a role did these new technological gadgets play, how big a push came from the greater demand for the company's products? Or was it either of those two considerations that really led to the decision? Was it rather the fact that the company had made big profits on past sales, had a lot of cash in the till, and saw no reason to pay out the cash to the stockholders instead of putting it into expansion? Or was it perhaps some executive's hunch that business was going to be enormous in a certain line—and his readiness to gamble on that hunch so that he would have the capacity to capture a bigger share of that business before any of his competitors got to it?

Though economists have tagged the swings in investment as the prime cause of short-term rises and declines of the economy, they have not been able to get a sure line on what causes the swings in investment. A great deal of theoretical and empirical research is probing into that question right now; economists clearly do not intend to give up in their effort to uncover the causes of cyclical swings in investment. Basically, their ideas divide into two categories:

1. *Accelerator theories.* These are based on the idea that a boost in demand for consumer goods works like an accelerator on the demand for investment goods. The accelerator effect varies, though, according to the level of business activity. If industry is operating far from capacity, the effect of, say, a 4 per cent increase in consumer demand upon business investment in new plant and equipment may be very small, or nil. But if industry is close to its preferred capacity rate or anticipates a crowding of its capacity ceiling, then a 4 per cent increase in consumer demand might mean as much as a tenfold jump in investment plans. The action of the accelerator also depends on business expectations; it will take a while before the new capacity comes on stream, and businessmen will want to be sure the market will still be there when they get their new plant.

2. *Financial theories.* These make investment depend chiefly on profits and on the availability and cost of capital. Profits are both an important source of internal funds for business investment and a strong incentive and guide (or, if profits are negative, a strong disincentive) to business-investment decisions. Similarly, plentiful and cheap capital will spur investment; tight and dear capital will drag it.

Making investment depend on profits and capital costs is the older theory; the accelerator idea came into general use with John Maynard Keynes's work in the 1930s. More recently, many economists have been getting back to the older notion that investment was primarily a function of past profits and on profit expectations as well.

Industry may make decisions to modernize its plant and equipment when it has no capacity problem. Indeed, the actual or anticipated pressure on profit margins may act as a great spur to such modernization and replacement programs, as it did in 1958. Recovery in capital spending in that recession year, well before industry was operating at, or near, preferred capacity rates, lends support to the financial rather than the accelerator theory. But the two ideas do not necessarily rule each other out. Nor do they rule out the independent thrust that came from technological innovations that made the investment in new types of equipment profit-producing (or at least profit-protecting). Despite the continuing hangover of excess capacity in nearly all sectors of the economy in 1959 and 1960, investment in new plant and equipment continued to move upward, thanks to modernization.

Nevertheless, the 1957–1958 recession and the two earlier postwar recessions have shown that investment is still a volatile element in our economy. Some degree of volatility appears inescapable in an economy in which investment decisions are made by individual businessmen rather than by a central planning authority. For in the American economy, the businessman plays the key role in bringing together and setting in motion the forces that make for growth.

Offsetting the swings

The booms and recessions that result from this volatility of investment are the price of a free economy. But government, of course, has come to play a bigger part in damping down the cyclical swings through discretionary monetary and fiscal policies, and through the built-in stabilizers: unemployment insurance, Old-Age and Survivors Insurance, and personal and corporate income taxes. On the whole, the economy's stabilizers appear to have worked well during the postwar period—so well, in fact, that while income from production fell fairly sharply in all three postwar recessions, consumption held firm, and the drops in investment soon reversed themselves. In the 1948–1949 recession, income from production dropped $14.8 billion, but consumption actually rose by $3.2 billion; in the 1953–1954 recession, income from production fell by $11.2 billion, and consumption again rose by $3.2 billion. In the sharper 1957–1958 recession, income from production declined by $16.9 billion, and consumption, for the first time in the postwar period, declined—but by only $0.9 billion.

Some economists, such as the late Sumner Slichter, have even concluded that the old business cycle has given way to a new pattern of "rolling readjustments," limited to one or a few sectors of a more diversified and stable economy. Most economists disagree: Mild recessions, they point out, have always been limited to certain sectors of the economy. They see no proof that recent recessions have been mild because they are limited, rather than limited because they have been mild. Back in 1924 and 1927, innocuous little recessions also gave rise to the notion that the vicious old business cycle was a thing of the past, and that we had entered a new era.

The real basis for the belief that we are unlikely to have another serious and prolonged depression is not that the structure of the economy has been so altered as to make such a depression impossible. It is, rather, the belief that, since the publication of Keynes's *General Theory of Employment, Interest, and Money* in 1936 and the revolution in economic analysis and policy it sparked, we have learned enough about contracyclical fiscal and monetary policy to restrain a runaway boom or to reverse a recession—and that any present or future administration would use those policy instruments to promote economic stability. The employment act of 1946 has made the promotion of economic stability a formal responsibility of our government.

Our main hope, then, is to stop recessions before they start—by preventing speculative booms; and if booms do develop and turn into sharp recessions, to switch monetary and fiscal policies around before they get out of hand. Yet there is a growing realization that fiscal and monetary policies are clumsy instruments, difficult to use. One major difficulty, of course, is knowing just when to switch and how far to go. Since our knowledge of the business cycle is limited, it is hard to be sure of just where we are at any given moment and what we can expect next. In the face of major economic trouble, political leaders and money managers would inevitably hesitate to advertise publicly that they feared a major break just ahead; that might assure that their fears would be realized.

So it appears inevitable that action to prevent a serious decline will be too little and too late. And there is at least some danger, as conservatives argue, that a later switch to much stronger action—involving very heavy budget deficits—would hurt business confidence and spending plans, and so largely offset its own aims. Effective use of the government's weapons will depend on public understanding and a belief that the government's measures are likely to help, not hurt, business.

The business community is not getting much of an education in these matters from political leaders or the financial press or businessmen's organizations. There are exceptions, such as the Committee for Economic Development and (if I may say so) *Business Week,* who have struggled manfully to explain these esoteric matters of contracyclical policy to the public—but with what success only the Lord knows. The myth of the annually balanced budget dies hard.

Combining stability and growth

In the short run, as we have seen, financial and economic factors—such as profits, cost and availability of capital, the course of sales in relation to the level of industrial capacity—determine swings in investment and the rate of economic growth. In the long run, the major forces determining growth are the cultural factors—science, technological progress, population trends, changes in social institutions.

The remaining job—and it's an incredibly difficult one—is to integrate the short run and the long run, the business cycle and the long-term growth trend.

For the economists, this means working out a unified growth theory. For the nation, it points to the possibility of a unified set of policies that could promote growth without so many unsettling short-term ups and downs.

The economists, thanks to pioneering work by Roy Harrod and Evsey Domar,[1] are moving toward such an integrated theory. It starts with the concept that the economy has, in any period of its history, a maximum, or "natural," growth rate which is determined by increases in the labor force and by technological progress.

That merely says that an economy can increase its real output (assuming that it is already functioning at full employment) only by adding more hands or by improving knowledge and techniques.

But there is nothing that guarantees that people or businesses will actually save and invest just the sums required to produce economic growth at this maximum rate. They may try to save and invest too little or too much.

Paradoxically, if they invest too much—in other words, try to achieve a growth rate beyond the economy's natural

[1] R. F. Harrod, *Towards a Dynamic Economy*, The Macmillan Company, New York, 1948; E. D. Domar, "Capital Expansion, Rate of Growth and Employment," *Econometrica*, vol. 14, pp. 137–147, April, 1946; *ibid.*, "Expansion and Employment," *American Economic Review*, vol. 37, pp. 204–217, March, 1947.

potential—that will cause economic stagnation. That is because the opposite face of excess saving and investment is too little consumption—and idle capacity. As idle capacity spreads, it brings a fall in investment and an increase in unemployment.

If planned saving is inadequate, however, the economy appears boomy. Consumers and businessmen are spending hot and heavy; existing plant and equipment are used intensively, and profits are high. But the price trend is inflationary, because people are spending too much, and there is not enough capacity to produce all the public wants.

Either way, it takes a dose of the opposite medicine to get the economy back on the track of its maximum, or natural, growth rate. If consumption is too high, the rate of saving would have to be stepped up—in order to free more resources for the production of capital goods; such increases in the economy's capacity to produce are what we truly mean by economic growth. And, as saving and investment climbed back to their desired rate, inflationary pressures would weaken and disappear, because the increased saving would be a curb on consumption, and at the same time the increased capacity would augment the supply of goods.

If, however, there is too much saving and too little consumption, with apparent overcapacity and a drag on employment and income, the aim would be to get people to spend more, and to reduce the over-all saving rate. The increased demand for goods would make existing capacity inadequate and thereby force expansions in productive capacity.

Chronic imbalance

Naturally, the ideal goal would be a steady balance, between growing consumption on one side and growing saving and investment on the other, that would permit the economy to expand at its maximum potential rate— the rate determined by expanding technology and the growing labor force—with neither inflation nor unemployment.

But a quasi-free economy like ours is not likely to strike that exact balance consistently, even with the government attempting to offset the shifts in demand and in saving and investment. Those shifts around a balance point constitute the familiar mechanism of the business cycle.

Much less familiar—but perhaps even more important —is another question. That is whether the real trouble with the American economy is that it has become chronically unbalanced on either one side or the other. Is it, for example, prevented from attaining its maximum growth rate by a chronic bias toward undersaving, overconsumption, and inflation? This would curb growth partly because inadequate savings mean inadequate investment, but also because inflation misdirects funds into the wrong channels —into such things as land speculation and bidding up prices of equities in the stock market, instead of productive investment. That the economy has a chronic tendency to undersave and overspend is the position taken by many conservative economists, bankers, and central bankers, including such men as William McChesney Martin, Jr., chairman of the Federal Reserve Board.

Or does our basic economic mechanism have a chronic set toward oversaving and too low a rate of income generation? Early in the 1957–1958 recession, Arthur Smithies of Harvard University summed up that case by saying: "The basic factor in the current recession is that the economy generates capacity faster than demand. Unless we have some powerful external stimulus as we had at the end of the war or during the Korean War, we tend to generate overcapacity. It's a persistent tendency of our economy." Smithies' view revives a position first developed by Alvin Hansen of Harvard in the 1930s—that a "mature" economy like that of the United States suffers from a dearth of investment opportunities, tends to oversave, and is therefore chronically underemployed. Hansen therefore favors "high pressure" economics, which will keep the economy moving forward a good head of steam from expanding demand. He denies that this will produce inflation. The American economy, Hansen believes, is not normally inflation-prone; it readily expands capacity and output to meet rising demand.

One can find plausible evidence in America's postwar experience to support either case. We have had chronic creeping inflation—which supports the overconsumption, undersaving, and underinvestment line. On the other hand, we have had—in recent years at least—a higher unemployment rate than during the earlier postwar years, and a tendency to generate overcapacity and to slip into fairly frequent recessions. This backs up the underconsumption, oversaving school.

Can both views be partly right? Or is it perhaps some other factor that has been disturbing the economy, causing us to have creeping inflation simultaneously with underconsumption, tendencies to a higher unemployment rate and to overcapacity—and slow growth?

One important possibility is that the economy has become far too rigid, immobile, and uncompetitive. One reason cited for this: that the growing power of big labor and big business has resulted in creeping inflation (which the Federal Reserve has sought to check by slowing the growth of the money supply) and in underemployment of human and material resources, except in the spurts sanctioned by the Federal Reserve during periods of recovery from recession. Another straitjacket on the economy comes from farm subsidies aimed at keeping up prices of farm products—and from other disguised subsidies, such as government stock piles of defense materials and tariff protections for particular industries.

These straitjackets might be loosened up by antitrust action, by new farm and labor legislation, by reducing government stock piles to more realistic levels, by greater foreign competition.

A second possibility is that it's the Federal government itself that is the real antigrowth villain. From this standpoint, government could be curbing growth in two different ways: (1) by refusing to consider a reduction in tax rates and (2) by refusing—with tax rates frozen at present levels—to permit adequate expansion in government spending.

There are strong reasons for thinking that we have reached a time when the American economy needs a boost of one sort or the other. For we have moved out of the postwar period into a new era in which, it now becomes increasingly clear, inflationary pressures have abated and growth is coming harder.

End of an era

In the period we have been through, there were enormous jobs of reconstruction to be done, and it was the American economy that was in a position to supply the goods that were so desperately needed elsewhere. The United States fed the world vast quantities of goods, materials, equipment, industrial techniques—and the gospels of increasing productivity and economic growth.

At the same time, we provided the bulk of armaments for the free world. From V-J Day to 1960 America gave other nations $77 billion, net, in government grants and credits—$25 billion in military aid, $52 billion in economic aid and grants of one type or another. This enormous outpouring of funds, unparalleled in history, did much to rebuild the war-shattered economies of many nations, including our former enemies, Germany and Japan.

As American-aided reconstruction was transformed into self-sustaining economic growth in other nations and international trade revived, the American economy received further stimulus from growing foreign demand.

Of course, we had enormous pressures for economic growth right here at home. This country had plenty of backlogs of its own to make up—backlogs accumulated not just during the war years, when production of civilian goods was tightly limited, but also during the long years of the Depression of the 1930s. After the war, America rapidly became a nation of homeowners, of middle-class suburbanites. Families were anxious to acquire automobiles, refrigerators, goods of all kinds—to match the rising tide of children.

The funds to finance all this were readily available. For there was a huge hang-over of liquid assets from the war, and, in the postwar years, the banking system continuously monetized the government's huge war debt. Credit was cheap and plentiful.

With such heavy domestic and international demand, backed by the growing supply of money and credit, prices crept up rather persistently. That price creep came to seem like one of the new conditions of life. Despite a good deal of moralizing about creeping inflation, however, few people thought it such a terrible hardship. For money incomes were rising faster than prices, and almost all other nations were suffering inflation at an even faster rate than the United States economy. Foreign demand for American goods seemed chronically greater than American demand for foreign goods; there was a widespread assumption that a permanent "dollar gap" existed.

Mounting demand produced not only creeping inflation but real growth as well. As demand pressed against
existing industrial capacity, business invested heavily in
new plant and equipment. And as job opportunities increased, the labor force expanded rapidly—particularly as
women were attracted from their homes into well-paid
employment. Farmers switched to industrial jobs by the
millions. Unemployment, the curse of the prewar years,
seemed almost forgotten, as the economy held to a re-
markably steady upward course, with only brief recessions
due basically to inventory adjustments and reductions in
government spending. One eminent economist referred to
the remaining unemployment as essentially of the "case"
variety, of more interest to social workers than economists
—the unemployment of people sick in mind, body, or
spirit, of people psychologically rooted to the ramshackle
towns or stony hills that they called home.

There had never been such prosperity, such rapid progress for so many people. Some social critics found it all too
much of a good thing, complained of a surfeit of honey, of
the evils of affluence. The case for continuously growing
production was derided as a piece of "conventional wisdom." [2]

This intellectual boredom with growth came just at the
point when growth itself began to come much harder,
when the easygoing and inflationary expansion of the postwar period was ending. During the 1957–1958 recession

[2] J. K. Galbraith, *The Affluent Society*, Houghton Mifflin Company,
Boston, 1958.

unemployment climbed to 7.5 per cent of the labor force—well above the "case level"—and persisted at 5 per cent or higher even during the recovery that followed that recession. In the last years of the 1950s it became clear that the United States had entered a period of adjustment to a new era in which the international balance of payments imposed discipline even on this country—an era of intense competition among the industrial nations—an era in which demand no longer pressed against the greatly expanded capacity limits of the American economy.

This adjustment was especially hard on the United States because the burden of armaments and aid programs was spread unevenly among the free world's industrial nations. In 1958 and 1959, the United States was shocked to find the famous dollar shortage rapidly becoming a dollar glut, as America's surplus in trade shrank and its aid programs and capital outflow to other nations continued at high levels. After running balance-of-payments deficits averaging little better than $1 billion a year from 1950 through 1956 (there was a small surplus in 1957, owing to Suez), the United States suddenly found out what it was like to be in balance-of-payments trouble. That year the United States ran a $3.4 billion deficit. Foreigners claimed $2.9 billion worth of it in gold; for the remainder they increased their dollar holdings.

This revived an old, almost forgotten fear—the fear that large-scale conversion of reserves and other liquid assets by foreigners could subject a nation to intense deflationary pressure, could threaten—in the case of a key currency such as the dollar—to topple the international financial structure.[3]

A postwar world that has, for so long, been dominated by inflation has almost forgotten what a liquidity crisis means. It is essentially the international version of, say, a company's liquidity crisis—a fear that it cannot meet its obligations with cash or near cash; a fear that the suspicious creditors will move in on it.

Basically, nations hold reserves of gold or foreign exchange for two reasons: as a means of settling short-term deficits in their over-all balance of payments and as a backing for their national currencies. As long as the economic weather stays fair and nations are able to keep their balance of payments reasonably under control—especially with the help of foreign aid or long-term loans or capital movements—their reserve base may shrink without causing appreciable trouble.

But if there is a severe shock to the economy of a major country, or a loss of confidence in its currency, nations that have been holding that key country's currency as reserves —as well as persons or companies holding "hot money"— may decide to get out of it. They will shift to what they think is a stronger currency, or to gold, for fear that, otherwise, they might not be able to meet their obligations or that faith in their own currency might weaken. As such fears are transmitted from nation to nation, restrictions on trade and exchange, devaluations and fears of devalua-

[3] See Robert Triffin, *Gold and the Dollar Crisis*, Yale University Press, New Haven, Conn., 1960, for a brilliant exposition of this problem.

tions mean a severe wrench to total economic activity—a push toward deflation—an aggravation of the forces of depression that brought on the liquidity crisis initially. Some economists believe that the collapse of the world's monetary system in 1931 was what turned a severe but essentially typical boom's-end drop into the worst, most persistent world-wide depression in economic history.

The necessity of preventing further deterioration in the balance of payments and of preventing gold from gushing out of New York provided an extra impetus to the determination of the Eisenhower administration and the Federal Reserve to fight inflation.

But, in 1959, just when the fear of inflation was at its height—when people everywhere were telling each other that the United States was facing permanent inflation and that investing in the stock market was the only way to beat it—the inflation threat waned. In part, this was due to the administration's restrictive budgetary policies, and to the Federal Reserve's restrictive monetary policies. But it was also due—perhaps even more fundamentally—to intensified foreign and domestic competition that stemmed from the brimming capacity of both foreign and domestic industry.

More ample United States productive capacity has militated against inflationary pressure in two ways: by holding down a splurge of investment aimed at expanding capacity and by making it possible for industry to meet demands while maintaining lighter inventories. The high cost of money also has caused companies to run relatively light on inventories, and to try to force their suppliers to carry inventories for them. This, in itself, reduces aggregate inventory requirements, since a central supplier can carry smaller stocks than a number of users would require separately. If the job of carrying inventories is forced all the way back on the manufacturer, he can reduce inventories further—by planning to meet schedules out of shifts in output, rather than by carrying inventory.

But it was not just United States capacity that had expanded. So had the capacity of foreign producers. World capacity in raw materials has become more than adequate, thanks to past investment and new substitute materials; the supply situation has become more than ample in coal, oil, copper, iron ore, rubber, coffee, tin, lead, zinc, and most other commodities. And the realization that stocks are ample and inflationary pressures negligible, has reduced demands for inventories further.

World capacity for producing industrial goods has also grown greatly, because of the world boom in plant and equipment investment in the 1950s. Although the period of growth was by no means ended, the world had acquired, by the end of the 1950s, far more ample facilities for producing steel, machinery, machine tools, chemicals, plastics, synthetic rubber, autos, construction machinery, man-made fibers, pharmaceuticals. Earlier, the world had looked to the United States for many of these things; now they not only were competing strongly in foreign markets, but they meant intense price competition for United States products in the domestic market.

At home, the demand for the output of United States industry seemed to have relatively little zip. Suspicions have grown among economists that the United States economy has been getting back to a state resembling Alvin Hansen's "stagnation" model—when investment opportunities were insufficient to absorb the savings that accumulated when the nation approaches full employment. Meanwhile, the deadlock of political forces had produced a virtual freeze on the level of government spending and on the structure of tax rates.

What to do

Many economists these days have moved to the conclusion that if we want faster growth, we must end the stalemate over United States fiscal policy and choose one or the other of two courses:

1. Government expenditures will have to be increased. Proponents of this course argue that a large and steadily growing volume of government spending could enable the economy to avoid stagnation—even if the national budget were always balanced, or were balanced on the average. Rising government expenditures have a feedback effect on income: Income grows, it produces more tax revenues (if tax rates are held constant), and government spending can rise still further.

2. Or taxes will have to be reduced, to give more scope to the growth of private spending. If the forces of growth in the private economy are just strong enough to permit total income to grow, provided that the government increases its spending in proportion to the increase in in-

come, but if national security needs do not dictate budget increases and pressure for nondefense spending fails to push total government outlays up sufficiently, then tax reduction would be in order. A number of observers, such as Herbert Stein, research director of the Committee for Economic Development, and James Duesenberry, of Harvard, think it quite possible that tax reductions will be too little and too late—because of the standoff of political forces competing for the kind of tax reduction they think favors their particular group. The result then would be a relatively low growth rate, with incomes sinking whenever private investment declined.

Of course, we could also try to accelerate the nation's economic growth by changing the tax *structure,* rather than by a general reduction in tax rates. There have been a great many proposals for such reforms in the treatment of depreciation allowances for capital assets, research expenditures, dividends, capital gains, the averaging over a period of years of individual income, and the liberalization of the treatment of business and capital losses.[4] Certainly, it is going to be a great deal easier to put through structural reforms within a pattern of general tax reduction (in which there will be "something for everybody") than in a situation where gains to one group of taxpayers will have to be offset by increased tax burdens upon others.

The choice of whether to cut taxes or boost government spending or to aim at some combination of both involves

[4] See Joseph A. Pechman's study for the CED, "Structural Changes in the Federal Tax System to Accelerate Economic Growth," Jan. 6, 1960, for a succinct review and critique of most of the proposed tax reforms.

economics; but it is also—perhaps even more—a matter of political and social preference. Conservative economists lean to the tax-cutting solution; liberal economists, to boosts in government spending. Many who are concerned primarily about the Soviet threat also lean to the second solution. For instance, M.I.T.'s W. W. Rostow told the Joint Economic Committee that "it is quite accurate to identify the Soviet advantage over the United States as consisting of a more stable percentage allocation to military and foreign policy sectors." [5]

The policy choice that emerges will depend on:

• External political pressures, especially Soviet-American relations, Communist Chinese moves, the problems of underdeveloped nations—in Africa and Latin America as well as in Asia. These pressures will affect the size and scope of many government programs, in defense, foreign aid, atomic energy, space exploration, and other lines.

• Internal political pressures—for welfare programs (social security, health, education, urban redevelopment, public transportation, agriculture, regional or "depressed area" problems, and so on) as against pressures for tax reduction. Even if the second push should be stronger, there would still be tough infighting over the kind of tax reduction needed under existing conditions—whether to aim it primarily at stimulating consumption or stimulating saving and investment, whether to give tax relief primarily to the lower income brackets or to the upper.

[5] See *Staff Report on Employment, Growth, and Price Levels,* Joint Economic Committee, 86th Congress, 1st Session, Dec. 24, 1959.

Ideology, interest, and leadership

In any case, ideology and personal or group interests are bound to affect the choice of growth policies finally arrived at. But so will the character and wisdom of political leaders who will have the task of developing growth policies to serve the interests of the nation as a whole, not just the aims of certain groups.

Can the American political process be trusted to work out solutions to these highly complex economic choices? It won't be easy.

But the United States has, for quite a long time now, been demonstrating that it can deal with long-range problems with more patience and consistency than its opponents or its friends—or even its own leaders—suspected. Even President Roosevelt apparently thought that United States public opinion would not permit American troops to remain in Europe long after World War II had ended; yet public opinion did permit this. At the war's end, few could foresee the Marshall Plan and other long-lasting programs to rebuild the world's shattered economy and to check the spread of communism in areas far from the United States; but they happened. And this country carried through these programs without basic change in its political and economic system.

The growth problem, too—crucial to the long-run survival of freedom in a troubled world—seems capable of solution in the typical undoctrinaire pragmatic American manner.

7

Why Research Spending Soars

The great thing the United States will have going for it in the years ahead will be the swift scientific and technological progress of our time—and a rising tide of investment resulting from American industry's new principle and practice of programmed innovation, creating a multiple flow of planned new products out of research in a new and powerful extension of capitalism's growth process.

Dominance of technology

How important this force is you can see by looking at the past impact of improving technology on output. Robert Solow of M.I.T. has estimated that, of the total increase in United States output per man-hour from 1909 to 1949, only 12.5 per cent was due to increase in capital equipment, while 87.5 per cent was due to technological progress.[1] In a second study, Solomon Fabricant of the National Bureau of Economic Research has found that, during the period 1871 to 1951, technological advance accounted for 90 per cent of the rise in output per man-hour, as against 10 per cent for capital formation.[2] And Benton F. Massell, in still a third independent study, done at the Cowles Foundation for Research in Economics, likewise has found that, during the period 1919 to 1955, technological change accounted for approximately 90 per cent of the rise in output per man-hour.[3]

In other words, it was not primarily more machinery in back of every worker, but an unknown combination of better machinery and technology, better organization, better management, and greater skills on the part of workers, that sent United States output soaring in the past half century.

The implications of these findings are of outstanding

[1] R. Solow, "Technical Change and the Aggregate Production Function," *The Review of Economics and Statistics*, vol. 39, pp. 312–320, August, 1957.

[2] S. Fabricant, "Resources and Output Trends in the U.S. since 1870," *American Economic Review*, vol. 46, May, 1956.

[3] B. F. Massell, "Capital Formation and Technological Change in United States Manufacturing," *The Review of Economics and Statistics*, vol. 42, pp. 182–188, May, 1960.

importance for policy makers and economists. They mean that the overwhelming emphasis of any program for growth must come to focus on technological progress— and the factors that promote it or obstruct it.

Once said, this may seem to be an obvious conclusion, one that "we have always known." Surely, you can find anticipations of these statistical measures of the impact of changing technology on output in the literature of the past two centuries. But the idea was never really built into the corpus of economic analysis or policy. Like many "new ideas" in economics, this new stress on the role of technology and research represents simply a shift of emphasis, perhaps a somewhat different way of looking at old knowledge—but a way that can be of crucial importance in reconstructing the economics of growth.

In the future, policy makers will have to concern themselves more with "the variables which govern the rate at which innovations are injected into the economic system than with the variables which determine the rate at which additions are made to the capital stock." [4] Such issues as expenditure by business on research and the policies of firms regarding the replacement of obsolescent equipment should come to be regarded as even more important than the rate of net investment.

Embarrassed economists

In particular, economists will have to rethink production theory. The discovery of the overriding importance of technological change should be, as Massell says, "... no

[4] *Ibid.*, p. 188.

small cause of concern, and possibly embarrassment, to economists," who have traditionally treated technology as lying outside the theory of production. Up till now, economists have simply assumed that capital, labor, and land (or subcategories of those factors) were the significant inputs, with technology taken as "given," in producing any output. An improvement in technology was simply represented by a shift in the production curve. This crude way of treating changes in production was perhaps satisfactory in the days of Ricardo when the "given" state of technological knowledge was relatively static, but it becomes meaningless, and seriously misleading, nowadays when technological change is swift and perpetual. But, whatever the past justifications, we are certainly in a strange state of analysis when the factors which are explicitly considered account for only 10 per cent of the increase in output per man-hour, and the remainder is attributed to an "outside" force, ". . . which is little understood, and about which we are able to offer little explanation." [5]

[5] *Ibid.*, p. 188. See also Wassily Leontief, "The Problem of Quality and Quantity in Economics," *Daedalus,* vol. 88, no. 4, pp. 622–632, Fall, 1959. Leontief finds some justification for economists to continue to focus upon the quantifiable inputs of "land, labor, and capital" in analyzing production, but adds: "The process of the gradual deepening and expansion of economic inquiry naturally brings it into closer contact with adjoining fields. Modern economics has established with technical-engineering disciplines a close cooperative relationship based on an effective division of labor. However, its borders with other social sciences are still very little explored. . . ." A full analysis of the production—and growth—process clearly lies far beyond the traditional boundaries of economics. See also Joan Robinson, "The Production Function and the Theory of Capital," *Review of Economic Studies,* vol. 21, 1953–1954, for a critique of the "static" assumptions of traditional production economics.

To stress the role of technological advance is, of course, not to deny that its impact upon the economy is largely communicated through the investment process. By and large, technological progress does not become "real" until it is embodied in new investment: Knowing how to plough a field faster does nothing until tractors replace horses. To be sure, changes in organization, techniques, and skills requiring little or no capital investment can also be important; and such new knowledge, similarly, means nothing until it is put to work. As one old farmer once told the expert from the university experiment station, "Hell, I ain't farming half as well as I know how already."

Generally speaking, however, an economy which is rapidly increasing its capital stock is also likely to be accelerating the process of technical advance. And that proposition has its converse: The rate of capital investment will be greatest when innovational change comes fastest—because the rate of profit will then also be high.[6]

Technology and stability

Technological advance should therefore help to keep an economy not only growing but also more stable. The reason is twofold: (1) Technological advance will be an underlying force for profit, for capital investment and for expansion—and an economy, like a bicycle, is more stable when it is rolling forward than when it is standing still; and (2) in periods of recession, the opportunities created by technological advance for profit-conserving investment, aimed at modernizing and replacing obsoles-

[6] B. F. Massell, *op. cit.*, p. 187.

cent equipment, will place a fairly high floor under capital investment—whose downswings have in the past been the main cause of recessions and depressions.[7]

But, in order to get the steady flow of investment in plant and equipment that results from technological progress, there must be regular and sustained efforts in research and development.

Rising R&D curve

To speed up technological progress, the curve of research and development expenditures in the United States keeps rising. In 1928, American industry spent less than $100 million on R&D. By 1953–1954, over-all research spending had jumped to more than $5 billion a year. In 1959, the total was $12 billion.[8]

To be sure, there is some question as to how much of this growth in R&D spending is due to inflation and changing definitions, and how much of it is real. Because of rising research costs, including both the salaries of researchers and costs of equipment and overhead, broader definitions and classifications of R&D outlays by industries and by the Department of Defense, changes in the reporting of research for tax reasons (the Revenue Act of 1954 gave corporations the right to "expense" R&D outlays), data in current dollars undoubtedly overstate the increase

[7] See "How and Why Industry Modernizes: A special Report to Management," *Business Week,* Sept. 27, 1958.

[8] The National Science Foundation (see Chart 5) put the R&D figure for 1959 at $11.16 billion, based on midyear data; the McGraw-Hill department of economics estimated the full-year total for 1959 as $12 billion (see Appendix).

Chart 5. Research and Development Expenditures, 1930–1960

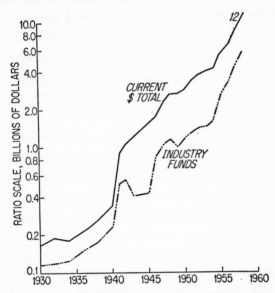

SOURCES: 1930–1940   Vannevar Bush, *Science the Endless Frontier*, p. 80
                    as adjusted in Steelman report, vol. I, p. 10.
         1941–1952   Department of Defense, *The Growth of Scientific
                    Research and Development*, p. 10.
         1953–1958   *Statistical Abstract of the U.S.*, p. 500, and National
                    Science Foundation, *Reviews of Data on Research
                    and Development*, nos. 1, 10, 13.
         1959–   Total figure of $12 billion estimated from National
                    Science Foundation data by McGraw-Hill Dept. of
                    Economics.

in real R&D outlays. Nevertheless, even when all the
"water" has been squeezed out of the research spending
figures, the rise has still been tremendous. David Novick,
head of the cost-analysis department of the RAND Corporation has adjusted the series on R&D spending by three

deflators—engineers' salaries, producers' durable equipment, and gross national product.[9] The results were not widely divergent; all reduced the actual growth by about one-half. Novick reported that the sixtyfold increase between 1930 and 1958 was cut to a twenty-five- to thirtyfold increase in real terms. But a thirtyfold increase (a 3,000 per cent increase, that is) cannot exactly be described as stagnation.

There is, furthermore, the question of whether these efforts to deflate the real increase in the volume of research and development work should not also be adjusted to take account of the increased productivity (that is, the changed quality) of both researchers and research equipment. If, through the use of computers, modern test equipment, and other devices, more highly qualified researchers are able enormously to increase their output, the dimensions of the real research effort—if it can be measured by the number and difficulty of the tasks undertaken and successfully executed—may have increased far more than even the unadjusted current dollar figures on research and development spending imply. It must be borne in mind that research is not a commodity like apples or pretzels that can readily be adjusted for price change; its output is knowledge, the value of which—especially over the long run—is incalculable.

Since *research* has become on "okay" word, applied to operations which produce no new knowledge, one cer-

[9] D. Novick, "What Do We Mean by Research and Development?" *California Management Review*, pp. 9–24, Spring, 1960.

tainly must try to distinguish the real rise from the phony. But one needs only one's naked eyes, regardless of what the imperfect data show, to reveal how the research revolution has transfigured the American scene. Go look at the research row stretching from Princeton, New Jersey, all the way into New York, at the research industries blooming along the Charles River and along the circumferential highway around Boston, at North Carolina's Research Triangle, at the laboratories and think factories of Los Angeles, San Francisco, San Antonio, upstate New York, Columbus, Wilmington, Washington, D.C., Chicago, Atlanta, and other centers. All around the country, sleepy old college towns have turned into boom towns where you are lucky to find a parking space or a table at the best restaurants—let alone a good house near the campus—because of the competition of the scientific and engineering elite that has engulfed those towns. In places like Cambridge, Princeton, and Palo Alto, the elite has become a mob.

And the research spending curve, which has done all this, will continue to rise. By 1969, according to a new McGraw-Hill study,[10] the R&D total will be more than $22 billion. Some observers put the future level of research spending still higher; Arthur D. Little, Inc., for example, has in an unpublished study projected an increase to approximately $35 billion by 1970. A. D. Little thus ex-

[10] Dexter M. Keezer, Douglas Greenwald, and Robert P. Ulin, "The Outlook for Expenditures on Research and Development during the Next Decade," here published as the Appendix, p. 213.

pected research expenditures to rise in the 1960s at about the same swift pace as in the 1950s—that is, approximately to triple in the decade. But the McGraw-Hill economics department expects some slowing in the rate of rise; total outlays, according to its projection, would increase a bit more than 80 per cent in the 1960s.

At some point, clearly, R&D spending must taper off— or else, as Guy Suits, vice-president and research director of General Electric, says, "... it would eventually constitute the entire economy—an anomaly that even the most partisan supporters of R&D would view with dismay." [11] United States business is already trying to determine the proper balance between research and development and other industrial functions, including capital investment, manufacturing, and marketing. The optimum combination of these interdependent activities, as Suits suggests, isn't a constant, but a variable that reflects changes in each industry and in the over-all economy brought about both by growth and by growing complexity.

Although any forecast of research expenditures will be subject to very wide ranges of error, one thing appears plain: The limit of the rise in the R&D curve is still a long way off.

Why the R&D curve rises

The most obvious (and doubtless the most fundamental) cause of the rise of research spending lies in the nature of

[11] C. G. Suits, "An Appraisal of Technological Progress," speech before the National Industrial Conference Board, New York, May 19, 1960.

scientific research itself. Research feeds upon itself: Discovery breeds discovery; innovation breeds innovation; and with each new discovery or innovation, the total body of scientific and technological knowledge increases.

Of course, this has always been so. But in our time the process has been accelerating.

The world has always had scientific and inventive geniuses. But frequently they were, as the common phrase has it, "ahead of their time." William Ogburn observed: [12]

> Leonardo da Vinci couldn't invent an airplane, although his brain was probably as good as those of the two bicycle repairmen who did invent it. But the materials for the airplane did not exist in da Vinci's day. The light gas engine was not invented until several centuries later. In the same way all scientific discoveries are built upon preceding scientific discoveries and are not something that comes fully created from the researcher's mind, as a result of only wishes and will power.

The thing that seems to be happening in our time is that all the once widely separated avenues of scientific and technological knowledge are converging, like the roads that lead into a city—a city where ideas are then swiftly exchanged, where civilization then swiftly grows.

Unlike the situation that confronted Leonardo, vast numbers of elements needed for further scientific and technological progress are now at hand, waiting for scientists and engineers to put them together. Miller B. Span-

---

[12] William F. Ogburn, "Technology and Planning," in George B. Galloway et al., *Planning for America*, Henry Holt and Company, Inc., New York, 1941, p. 176.

gler [13] has categorized these elements—which he calls "building blocks"—in this way:

1. Process materials—metals (including "new" metals like uranium, titanium, beryllium), alloys, plastics, laminates, fuels, chemicals, fibers, clay, etc. New or improved process materials frequently lead to technological changes in many industries where cost saving is involved.

2. Process equipment—turret lathes, boring mills, planers, milling machines, gear cutters, grinders, welding machines, forges, deep-drawing presses, centrifuges, agitators, ball mills, boilers, condensers, compressors, jet-molding machines, glass-blowing machines, extrusion dies, rolling mills, billeting machines, cyclotrons, etc. New models of these machines are capable of greater speeds and precision than those of only a decade ago. Automatic or semiautomatic operation of these machines has led to large cost reductions. New process equipment may result from new process materials—for instance, metallurgical advances may permit the construction of machinery of greater durability, or permit its operation under greater ranges of temperature and pressure.

3. Tools of measurement and observation—chronometers, compasses, sextants, telescopes, microscopes, pressure gages, thermometers, calorimeters, micrometer calipers,

[13] Miller B. Spangler, *New Technology and the Supply of Petroleum: The Treatment of Uncertainty in Resources Planning*, Research Paper No. 2, The University of Chicago, Program of Education and Research in Planning (RFD #1, Yorktown Heights, New York: The Author, 1957), 299 pp. This is a study of outstanding insight and imagination.

protractors, planimeters, levels, plumbs, transits, spring scales, analytical balances, volumeters, ammeters, wattmeters, oscilloscopes, conductivity bridges, thread gages, surface gages, sine bars, hydrometers, anemometers, polarimeters, spectrometers, spectroscopes, gravimeters, magnetometers, surface tensiometers, viscosimeters, torquemeters, vibrometers, X rays, polariscopes, Nicol prisms, photometers, Wilson cloud chambers, Geiger counters, seismographs, etc. These have importance in many industrial applications, such as exploration or quality control or automatic operations, but their most significant use is in scientific and industrial research itself. New and better instruments lead to new experiments—and whole series of scientific discoveries and industrial innovations.

4. Calculating devices—adding machines, electronic computers, mathematical tables such as trigonometrical functions, random numbers, Poisson distributions, nomographs, Mollier diagrams, fugacity charts, entropy and enthalpy charts. New calculating devices enormously reduce the costs of research, make it possible to solve problems which formerly were simply too expensive and time-consuming to tackle. The greatest importance of these devices probably is that they astronomically expand the productivity of scientific investigators.

5. Recording devices—photographic equipment, sound-recording equipment, microfilm, memory tapes, geophones, time recorders, temperature recorders, pressure recorders, volume-of-production recorders, etc. These improve pro-

duction control and facilitate automation. Improved handling of statistical and engineering information accelerates research and development.

6. Instruments of communication—telegraph, telephone, radio, television, intercom systems, teletype, radar, photoelectric cells, dictaphones, signaling devices, sirens, limit switches, alarms, moving pictures, etc. These permit the swift interchange of ideas and information from human to human—and from machine to machine. The growth of electronics, which we looked at in Chapter 4, brings advance in this communications area at a fantastic rate—and removes the cost deterrents to their use in many industrial applications.

7. Inventories of standardized items—wrenches and repair tools, nuts and bolts, chemicals, batteries, condensers, transistors, valves, motors, pumps, folk lifts, etc. These minimize delay in fabrication and repair, and reduce the costs of industrial processes and of research and development work.

8. Reference literature—encyclopedias, dictionaries, bibliographies, indexes, technical books, handbooks, periodicals, trade journals, etc. These stores of information are of enormous importance to the scientist and engineer. Accounts of previous experiments, experiences, and observations are essential if the scientist is to keep abreast of his field, be alert to opportunities for additional research, and avoid duplication in research. As Spangler notes, "A basic part of scientific training is to learn the particular literature sources of data and facts too numerous to commit

to memory. The continual revision of data and the growth of scientific knowledge greatly enhance the utility of these building blocks of technological progress." [14] In fact, the enormous difficulties of keeping up with the work in one's own field (which requires the assistance of growing numbers of exceptionally well-qualified librarians and editors and teachers), together with the essentiality of having access to the enormous apparatus required for scientific and technological research in so many areas today, is the basic force behind the shift from the individual investigator to the research team, from the bicycle shop to the large industrial or government or university research center. This shift need not mean debasement of the individual intelligences and imaginations required—but it does imply greater specialization, and more emphasis upon communication and cooperation among the specialists.

"Groupthink"?

Although some outsiders (including many economists and sociologists and social critics) seem to feel that the move toward the team approach in research is somehow a reactionary move—an instance, perhaps, of George Orwell's "groupthink"—the more gifted investigators appear to be drawn to large institutions where they can find skills and talents complementary to their own and where the resources will be adequate to permit the researcher to tackle critical problems with some hope of success. Studies which emphasize the great contributions made in the past

[14] *Ibid.*, p. 80.

by individual inventors as proof of the individual's supe-
riority over the team [15] would appear to have limited application to the present or the future. This is of course
not to say that, in all fields, the day of the individual researcher or inventor is gone; there doubtless are still many
opportunities for the lone thinker to make tremendous
contributions in mathematics, theoretical physics, symbolic
logic, economics, etc., as well as in the area of practical
gadgetry. In any case, the argument about the merits of
the individual researcher versus the research team is somewhat meaningless—for individuals in the sciences are
simply not "alone"; they depend upon the enormous heritage of Western science, language, and civilization—and
they are fools if they do not keep up and benefit from what
colleagues in their own field or related disciplines are
doing. In the sciences and social sciences, the pro is separated from the crank—generally speaking—by knowing
what others have already done and are now doing.
Whether investigators operate best from the vantage point
of a university campus or an industrial laboratory or on
their own depends partly on the choice of research problems, partly on personal taste and preferences.

In any event, the enormous expansion of scientific and
technical endeavor, utilizing the building blocks of new
materials, new tools of measurement and observation, new
calculating devices, recording devices, instruments of communication, standardized parts, and catalogued stores of

[15] See, for instance, J. Jewkes, "How Much Science?" *The Economic
Journal,* vol. 70, no. 277, pp. 1–16, March, 1960.

ancient and recent information and ideas, makes it virtually certain that we are still in the *early* phase of our research revolution.

With so many interrelated elements being brought to
bear on research problems today, Spangler suggests that
the probability of further technological progress—of continuing scientific break-throughs and economic innovations—is very high, because of the operation of the "law of
large numbers." [16]

Applied to research work, this simply means that there
is some truth probability to the statement "Seek and ye
shall find." Spangler has sought to find a way of mathematically estimating the probabilities of a successful out-
come at every stage of the road from fundamental knowledge, to theoretical solution, to technological solution, to
economic solution, of research problems, in order to get
an idea of the future rate of innovation.

While such probability estimates lead to "pessimistic"
conclusions about the chances of achieving any particular
innovation (meaning an *economic* solution), the law of
large numbers leads to "optimistic" conclusions about
the chances for *over-all* technological progress: [17]

> The *average* ratio of success of the research projects
> to be completed in the next several decades can safely be

---

[16] The law of large numbers maintains that the larger a random sample
is, the more closely will it resemble the characteristics of the population
from which the sample was drawn. This is sometimes called "the law of
averages."

[17] *Ibid.*, p. 94.

assumed to be *at least as great* as that experienced in the past several decades. As the quality of scientific personnel improves and with increased expenditures for research, the average success ratio may even improve.

The rate of progress will also depend upon whether we put our intellectual and financial resources into the right places—and that may well require a shift of resources from applied toward fundamental research—if we want to step up the number of innovations we eventually get out of the business end of the R&D pipeline. The real bottleneck is at the beginning, not at the end, of the research process.

Industry is becoming more and more aware of the necessity of that shift to basic research. Before World War II, very little fundamental research originated in industrial laboratories; scientists in the universities were in fact constantly astonished to learn that any "pure" research was done in any industrial laboratory.[18] And most university men thought that a concern with the practical usefulness of fundamental research was rather vulgar or even sinful; and that notion persists in some quarters, though it is changing, as the urgent importance of science for industry, government, and economic development becomes more widely understood by scientists.

And since World War II, business has begun to regard basic research as a practical and economic investment for industrial growth. The McGraw-Hill survey of research expenditures found that, in 1959, United States industry was spending $270 million on basic research—compared with

[18] Suits, *op. cit.*, p. 13.

$5 million in 1945.[19] That industrial investment of $270 million in basic research in 1959 constituted 29 per cent of all dollar expenditures on *basic* research in this country. This is, of course, not to say that the total outlay of $960 million on basic research, out of a total R&D expenditure of $12 billion, is adequate. It probably is not. Indeed, the McGraw-Hill data show that industry's percentage allocation of funds to basic research has diminished from 4 per cent of total R&D outlays in the earlier postwar years to 3 per cent now, though in absolute terms the rise in basic research spending by industry has been great.

It would be a mistake to underestimate the significance of industry's new-found interest in basic research, or of the results that have already begun to flow from it. Literature studies by General Electric researchers show that the industrially contributed fraction of basic-science publication amounts to 19 per cent in the field of physics (including all subdivisions), in chemistry to 22 per cent, and in metallurgy and ceramics (combined) to 37 per cent.[20]

Government laboratories have also been making significant contributions to the output of basic research. The same General Electric study shows these contributions by government laboratories: in physics, 22 per cent; in chemistry, 15 per cent; and in metallurgy and ceramics, 20 per cent. University contributions were 56 per cent in physics, 59 per cent in chemistry, and 35 per cent in metallurgy and ceramics.

Of course, one cannot be sure whether this is or is not

[19] See Appendix, Table 5.
[20] Suits, *op. cit.*, p. 13.

a fair division of the fundamental research burden among industry, government, and the universities. One might even argue that industry should be *less directly* involved in basic research (while spending more on basic research via grants to universities and other research institutions), should not be seducing fundamental researchers from the campuses, where they can choose their tasks more freely, without any commercial direction. It is at least possible that science and technology expand optimally when they grow by their own "inner logic," without any concern about proximate or ultimate goals. That old argument still goes round and round inconclusively; it is a general "philosophical" argument that doubtless can only be settled by detailed examination of the particulars in many fields; the universities may or may not be the most fertile and vital sources of new fundamental knowledge in every area. In some areas, industry and the government are probably moving in to fill a vacuum; profits and political necessities can be energizing forces even in basic research. In many areas (especially those related to national security problems) the lines between industry, government, and the universities have in any case been smudged almost out of existence.

Mighty role of government

The United States government is, by far, the major source of funds for research and development work.[21] In 1959, the government put up $7.2 billion—or 60 per cent

[21] See Appendix, Table 1.

of total R&D outlays. (Private industry provided $4.6 billion, or 37 per cent of the total; colleges and other institutions provided $300 million, or only 3 per cent of the total). Most of the funds the government put up went to finance R&D work by private industry and research institutions; of the $7.2 billion total provided by government, $4.6 billion went to industry, $1 billion to colleges and other institutions—and only $1.6 billion was spent in government laboratories. And of the $7 billion the government provided, $6 billion went for research in defense and defense-oriented industries.[22]

Most research prognosticators today believe that, although the government's annual investment will probably not increase much in the decade ahead, it will probably not decrease much either.[23] The reason lies in the role Federal spending has come to assume in basic research.

Basic research, especially in some of the newer fields of physical science—solid-state physics, cryogenics (cold-temperature research), plasma research, electronics, hypersonics, and so forth—costs big money. Except for the very largest companies, few individual corporate budgets are big enough to support this highly risky research investment; the probability of success in cases of individual projects—as Spangler's mathematical reasoning suggests—is pretty low. But the results of successful gambles may be

[22] But the results of such research might have important civilian applications.

[23] Jane Cutaia, "The Impact of Research on the Corporation," address to Public Relations Society of America, Mar. 15, 1960; see also Appendix, pp. 218–225.

so tremendously valuable not just to industry but to the nation and its security that the risks of investment in research should be socially borne. For the probability of *some* rich strikes among the total volume of research endeavors, owing to the law of large numbers, is good. This conclusion need not, however, rest on probability analysis: various wartime research efforts—the development of radar, synthetic rubber, and the atomic bomb, to name just three—demonstrated that almost any scientific problem can be solved if enough high-powered, organized scientific brain power is directed at it. With so many big scientific and technological problems set out before us as a nation—everything from the building of a more secure national defense to deter Communist attack, to exploring space, to solving the resource and urban and transportation problems created by population growth—there is every reason to expect that heavy Federal support of R&D will continue.

Industrial financing of research

It would, however, be a serious mistake to exaggerate the degree to which the continuing rise in research spending depends on government support. Of the $9.1 billion in R&D work performed by industry in 1959, industry itself did, after all, provide half the financing. And that $4.5 billion spent by industry on R&D in 1959 was more than twice as much as industry put into research in 1953, more than four times as much as it invested in research in 1946.[24]

[24] Table 1, Appendix.

The chief reason for this trend is simple but dramatic: Much of United States industry has caught on, with a bang, to the proposition that research produces innovations and innovations produce profits—either by creating or expanding markets or by cutting costs.

Research, profits, and growth

Since World War II, the most profitable industries and companies, and the ones with the best growth records, have been those that had an outstanding performance in research and innovation. The importance of the research-profit-growth nexus has been sharply pointed up by a study of fifty large industrial companies by AT&T.[25] This study clearly showed that, as between different industries or between companies within the same industry, the research-minded companies tended to be the most profitable. One cannot, of course, lay out a simple cause-effect (or chronological) sequence leading from research to profit to growth. Some would make profit the initiating factor. Some would put far more emphasis on good management. Some would give more weight to shifts of demand upon particular companies or industries from outside political, demographic, or technological forces. The causes of company profit and growth are obviously highly complex. Nevertheless, some of AT&T's case histories reveal that research can in fact frequently be isolated as the critical cause of a company's profits and growth.

[25] W. M. Larrabee et al., *Profit, Performance, and Progress*, American Telephone and Telegraph Co., New York, 1959.

For instance, the AT&T study contrasts the performance of International Business Machines Corp. with two other, unnamed companies—both of which had larger sales than IBM just before World War II. All three companies prospered through the war and the period of high postwar demand immediately after the war. But, in 1951, IBM saw tougher competition ahead and decided to boost its already substantial research expenditures, though this meant lower profits in the short run. IBM's heavy investment in research led to new and improved products, more rapid growth, and higher profits in the long run.

Meanwhile, the other two companies tried to grow by buying other companies, rather than by finding and making better products. As the 1950s wore on, they fell farther and farther behind. Finally, one started a crash program, pouring back into research a larger part of each sales dollar than any other company in the industry, hoping to get back in the running; the other company, the AT&T study said, "... is now so poor it cannot devote much money to research." AT&T concluded mournfully: "It is going to be difficult to restore this company to financial health."

Such cases—and they can be found in other industries—are what lie behind the change in management thinking about the importance of R&D. More and more companies have come to regard expenditures for research not as a luxury but as a necessity to meet both domestic and foreign competition; many executives have come to refer to research as the lifeblood of successful business operation.

Wall Street has learned to keep a close watch on a company's research activities; that a company has a strong and productive research program has come to be one sure way of judging management's competence and the company's growth prospects.[26]

Indeed, so spectacular have been the results of research that "research" has been used, by some sharp operators or faddists, as a gimmick. The Jem Flatiron Co. has become Jemtronics, and National Cowbell has become Bovisonics. Alas, hypocrisy is the homage that vice offers to virtue, as La Rochefoucauld said.

But real research will go on expanding—thanks to the logic of science, the quest for profits, and the awful responsibilities facing our government.

[26] The impact of research on company growth and profits is well illustrated by the performance of such companies as Aerojet-General, American Telephone & Telegraph, Baxter Laboratories, Bendix Corp., Brush Beryllium, Corning Glass Works, Dow Chemical, Du Pont, Eastman Kodak, Eli Lilly, Fansteel Metallurgical, Firestone Tire & Rubber, Foote Mineral, General Dynamics, General Electric, General Telephone & Electronics, B. F. Goodrich, Haloid Xerox, International Business Machines, International Telephone & Telegraph, Merck, Minneapolis-Honeywell, Minnesota Mining & Manufacturing, National Cash Register, North American Aviation, Owens–Corning Fiberglas, Chas. Pfizer, Phillips Petroleum, Polaroid, RCA, Rohm & Haas, Schering, G. D. Searle, Shell Oil, Smith, Kline and French Laboratories, Sperry Rand, Texas Instruments, Thiokol Chemical, Thompson Ramo Wooldridge, Union Carbide, United Aircraft, U.S. Rubber, Upjohn, Vick Chemical, Western Union, and Westinghouse. These are described in *R&D and the Investor*, Merrill Lynch, Pierce, Fenner & Smith, New York, 1960.

8

War, Peace, and the Research Revolution

"God takes care of children, drunkards, and the United States." There's always been consolation in that cracker-barrel philosophy for a nation that thinks it's a special case—a nation that hates to be distracted from its own business and pleasures—a nation that can't believe it can really be hurt, until it is.

In the past there has always been time to snap out of it and to respond—swiftly and devastatingly—to attack.

But is the threat to America today different from those of the past? Are we involved in the kind of struggle which, if we cannot win in a few months or years of all-out effort, we shall gradually lose? Has America at last come up against an opponent who knows how to exploit this democracy's greatest weaknesses—its preoccupation with domestic and personal affairs, its tendency to live from day to day and not to plan ahead to achieve any specific national objectives, its dislike of politicians and of government itself, its chronic optimism and refusal to believe that things are as bad as they look? In the past, in ordinary times, these traits were forgivable—perhaps even praiseworthy. But these are not ordinary times.

The gravest problem for America in this struggle between democracy and dictatorship is that many Americans are hardly awake to the struggle. They find it hard to see what the fuss is all about. There's much confusion, therefore, about what sacrifices, if any, must be made to win the struggle—and much uncertainty, even among those who are fully aware of what's at stake, as to how a free society, with an unplanned economy, can mobilize for a conflict that may last for decades.

A new problem

Not only the United States but the entire world is facing a historically unprecedented problem—a problem that was created by the research revolution.

The nature of that novel problem is this:

A state of conflict exists between the great powers. The

Communists, led by the U.S.S.R., have declared their intention to make a world revolution; the non-Communist powers, led by the United States, have declared their determination to prevent this. In the past, force—and the threat of force—played a major role in resolving or freezing such national or ideological conflicts. At present there is no substitute for the threat of force in sight for this end. But the forces that each side can use today—or, possibly, tomorrow, when the stage of invulnerable long-range rockets with H-bomb warheads is fully reached—are so terrible that no power that goes to war could hope to survive that war. It is highly probable that any major war between the great powers would become a nuclear war— even if nations first got rid of all existing nuclear bombs. For the world can no longer rid itself of the knowledge of how to make nuclear bombs; and nations might be driven to put that knowledge to use, rather than go down into total and final defeat.

Thus far, this novel situation created by the research revolution has given the world a remarkable degree of stability, given the scope and intensity of the world conflict. Despite twenty-two brush-fire wars, ranging up to the size of Korea, and nearly half a hundred revolutions, including the Chinese, there has been no major war between the great powers. But there is no peace, either, and none is in sight. For the roots of conflict between the Communists and the free world exist, and they will not disappear until either the Communists give up their revolutionary ambitions or until the West submits.

That leaves the United States, the Soviet Union, and the world facing this dilemma: In the years ahead the threat of force will continue to be indispensable. But the actual use of force is almost certain to be suicidal.

This is not a dilemma that makes for easy sleeping. It involves terrifying uncertainties for both sides.[1] There are the dangers of surprise attack: A nation, if it thought it could get away with an attack that would knock out most of another nation's retaliatory power, might take the gamble.

There are the dangers of accidental war: It has been said that, under some circumstances, a flight of geese or a rain of meteors showing upon a radar screen might mean the end of the world. Technical experts from the military say this is highly unlikely, that adequate checks exist to prevent it. Still, no one denies that there are real dangers of accidental war resulting from political events—from a miscalculated gamble on Berlin, say, or on Formosa.

And there are the dangers of provocation. Nation A might tempt nation B to attack nation C, so that nation B would finally get into a war and could be knocked out, without danger to nation A. President de Gaulle of France has spoken of the "melancholy circumstances" in which the United States might wipe out Eastern Europe and the Soviet Union might wipe out Western Europe. In strategic thinking, this would be a massive instance of the tit-for-tat threat.

[1] See Herman Kahn, *The Nature and Feasibility of War and Deterrence*, 86th Cong., 2d Sess., Document 101, Jan. 20, 1960.

De Gaulle's solution to this problem, obviously, has been to get nuclear arms of his own to deter attacks on his own nation. But this leads to compounding the instability, as other nations are driven to do the same thing.

This is what the specialists refer to as the nth-country problem. They mean that the United States was the first country to have the bomb, the Soviet Union the second, Britain the third, and so on, until a decade from now, when the nth country will have it.[2] The instabilities are great enough when only a few countries have these ultimate weapons, but when virtually all countries acquire them (and the economic costs of doing that, the experts say, will be quite modest for a nation in the decade ahead), the dangers of war from surprise attack, accident, or provocation—possibly anonymous provocation—will become enormous. With Red China as a possible nth country, even the boldest planners must suffer nightmares, both in Washington and in Moscow.

Communist strategy

The bomb thus creates a nice problem for the Communist revolutionists: How can they achieve their world revolution without blowing up the world and themselves in the process?

Actually, the Communists have a strategy designed precisely to get round this problem. This is the strategy of "protracted conflict," which postpones the decisive battle

[2] See *Establishing International Control of Nuclear Testing*, National Planning Association, Special Report No. 50, July 21, 1958.

against an excessively dangerous and heavily armed opponent (such as the United States) and scales each attack upon that opponent to the risks involved—until the balance of power has shifted overwhelmingly to the side of the revolutionary forces.[3] The chief characteristics of this strategy of protracted conflict are: (1) the adherence to the total and final objective—sometimes stated in honeyed, sometimes in brutal terms by Khrushchev ("My lttle doves, you must all become Communists.... We are confident of the final victory of communism.... We will bury you....") and (2) the shrewdly selected and controlled means to achieve that total objective—"... the constant shifting of the battleground, weapons systems and operational tactics for the purpose of confusing the opponent, keeping him off balance and wearing down his resistance." [4]

---

[3] A study by the Foreign Policy Research Institute, Robert Strausz-Hupe et al., *Protracted Conflict*, Harper & Brothers, New York, 1959, has brilliantly analyzed this strategy. The writers find that "... it is—and always has been—the strategy of the Russian and Chinese Communists, who have been able not only to accept but even to thrive upon conflict as the normal condition of the twentieth century." The strategy has been described by Mao Tse-tung in his book *On the Protracted War*. The Communists in this and in many other books and speeches—and deeds—have revealed their over-all designs as frankly as Hitler did in *Mein Kampf*. We tend to disbelieve such proclaimed schemes for conquest. Pietro Quaroni, formerly the Italian Ambassador to Moscow, has said: "We should always give careful attention to what the Russian leaders say: they have the good, or bad, habit of always telling us the truth. When I say, 'the truth,' I should add that we must understand clearly what various words, such as peace, freedom, and so on, mean in the Communist jargon. But it is not difficult to understand this meaning; it is sufficient merely to study the sacred writings of Communism cursorily: they are all at our disposal.... But we want to disbelieve it, particularly so when it interferes with our own ideas." (P. Quaroni, "East and West and the Summit Conference," a lecture to the Free University of Berlin, 1959.)

[4] Strausz-Hupe, *op. cit.*, p. 2.

This strategy for wiping out an opponent over a period of time alternates limited thrusts, feints, and threats with seductive invitations to make peace; it uses psychological, economic, political, cultural means; and—whenever the time is opportune—direct violence. The Communist has many pieces to play, and he is in no hurry to get up from the board. The threat of the bombs in our hands keeps him patient.

To be sure, Communist patience might suddenly disappear if they were to gain a decisive advantage in the technology of mass destruction—or a defense against existing technologies. The strategy of protracted conflict by no means rules out the total knockout blow—if the Communists could deliver it without being destroyed themselves.

Of course, there are differences within the Communist camp—between factions within Russia and between the present Russian and Chinese leaders—as to the choice and timing of military, political, economic, and psychological means for achieving the revolutionary end. Soviet neo-Stalinists and the Chinese leaders have invoked the teachings of Lenin to prove that a cataclysmic world war between communism and capitalism is inevitable; but the leader of the Soviet bloc, Khrushchev, warns [5] the Communists against "mechanically repeating what Lenin said many decades ago" and asserts that world revolution will be achieved through his policy of "peaceful coexistence."

> History will possibly witness such a time when capitalism is preserved only in a small number of states.... Well?

[5] *The New York Times,* June 26, 1960, p. E3.

> And even in such conditions would one have to look up in a book what Lenin quite correctly said for his time, would one just have to repeat that wars are inevitable since capitalist countries exist?... One must not only be able to read but also correctly apply it in the specific conditions of the time in which we live....

Khrushchev obviously feels confident that the United States and the countries allied to it are weakening, politically, economically, and psychologically, and that Communism can triumph without running the risk of a ghastly war that perhaps no one will survive. Khrushchev's policy of peaceful coexistence is thus one that foresees a period in which a shrinking number of capitalist states and a growing number of Communist states will live side by side, a transitional period in which communism will be the strong, healthy force of the future and capitalism the sick, decadent survivor of the past, condemned by history, communism's substitute for God, to extinction. But the old capitalist regime can make trouble with its terrible weapons; better let it die in bed—if possible help it along toward the grave in any way that comes to hand and won't provoke a dangerous outburst.

The Chinese Communists talk less patiently and "moderately." Their party organs declare that United States imperialism must be beaten "black and blue," that an "unjust war launched by United States imperialism" must be countered by a "just war." The Chinese know, however, what they are up against; their papers declare that it is "not easy" for anyone to dare to struggle against the United States with its huge military equipment and atomic weapons. But they say the United States is a "brittle paper tiger," and it can be defeated. Red Chinese political leaders and generals admit that weapons are important but declare "it is still man, not material, that is the decisive factor in modern war." They say that "modern revisionists" (meaning Khrushchev and his followers) have "exaggerated the consequences of the destructiveness of nuclear war."

It is unlikely that the Chinese leaders believe their own propaganda or are as rash and contemptuous of American military power as they pretend. Certainly, their actions have been more cautious than their words; following the strategy of protracted war, of which Mao Tse-tung is the leading theorist, they have in fact calibrated their attacks to the risks involved, have avoided moves certain to bring American nuclear power into action.

Living dangerously

As I write, in the summer of 1960, the Russians have cynically and insultingly broken up the Geneva conference on disarmament. This was consistent with their behavior since Khrushchev torpedoed the Summit conference in Paris. What's behind the 180-degree turn in the Russian line since the now-long-dead "spirit of Camp David" is best known to the men in the Kremlin. Was it the American refusal to give up Berlin or any other important object of Communist ambition? Was it pressure from neo-Stalinists in Russia or from the fire-eating Chinese Communists—possibly aggravated by the U-2 affair and its disclosure of Soviet vulnerability to air-borne attack?

Whatever the nominal cause or combination of causes,

one thing is clear: There is still no hope of reaching agreement with the Communists on disarmament or any other important issue dividing East and West through an approach based on sweet reason or good will. The Soviets are prepared to negotiate only so long as the West is willing to give up what the Communists want, while the Communists give up nothing. The conflict between the Communists and the West cannot be resolved so long as they are still driving hard for world revolution, except on terms of abject surrender.

Once again we have learned that the crazy-seeming swings in the Communist line, which we have seen for so many years (the swing from fighting the Nazis in Spain to the Molotov–von Ribbentrop pact to the holy war against the Hitlerites was just one example), are perfectly consistent tactical moves within the strategy of protracted conflict.

However unpleasant these facts of life in the twentieth century may be for those who had begun to hope that some agreements with the Russians could be reached that would reduce the dangers of war, there is no reason to grow overly despondent over the collapse of the Geneva talks on disarmament and over the Summit failure before it, or alarmed about the possible imminence of war. For the history of the cold war shows that the Communists do in fact show a reasonable and proper understanding of the limits to their aggression imposed by America's strength.

The breakdown of the Geneva conference obviously is not the end of our quest for peace—for peace with justice and freedom. It clearly does mean that, to achieve such peace, we must maintain and develop our armed strength, not be misled by the illusion that expressions of good will can persuade the Communists to be gentlemen and stop trying to push us off this planet.

We have learned once more that the Communists respect only one thing—power; and we must make them respect ours even more. That is why we must maintain and increase our military strength—our bases, missiles, bombs, satellite detection systems, and all the other awesome creations of the research revolution. These, ironic as it may sound, are the real forces for peace in our time.

For the United States must continue to enforce international order through its deterrent power. This means that the United States must develop an invulnerable "second-strike" power, in the language of the military experts: a family of long-range missiles invulnerable to an enemy's first strike—because our missiles would be under the sea in submarines in unknown locations, or on railroad cars touring the country, or in "hardened" underground bases. Then any nation that struck the United States—no matter how terrible the blow—would be certain to be destroyed itself. The United States is well on the way to building this second-strike force around four long-range missiles—the Atlas, the Titan, the Polaris, and the Minuteman.

To avoid provoking war, we shall have to make it continuously clear to the Communists that we have no intention of striking first, but that we would certainly strike back against a nuclear attack with devastating effect. The number of missiles we need to do this deterrent job is not very great—it might run in the hundreds or low thousands —owing to the fantastic destructiveness of the nuclear war heads and the accuracy of the missiles. The second-strike missile force has to be just large enough to prevent any nation from trying a first strike against us.

We shall have this invulnerable second-strike deterrent within the next few years; some elements of it are already operational. Until that force is fully ready, we must continue to rely on manned aircraft, operating from forward bases, aircraft carriers, or strategic bases within the United States, to deter enemy aggression.

But we must not be misled into exaggerating the degree of stability that our present military technology ensures or be beguiled by that word *invulnerable*—which might have a time dimension. New technological break-throughs by the enemy could upset the present balance of terror; the research revolution makes that a constant possibility. In fact, as Possony has said, "The rapidly accelerating technological race is the essence of the conflict...." [6]

For years to come, we shall have to rely on information and intelligence systems and on R&D work to forestall enemy surprises in operations or in technology. This technological competition—which makes laboratories and testing grounds the critical theater of the world conflict—will not be restricted to the area of nuclear war. If we are to

[6] Stefan T. Possony, "Review of Nuclear Weapons and Foreign Policy by Henry A. Kissinger," *Annals of the American Academy of Political and Social Science*, vol. 316, p. 141, March, 1958.

counter Communist military moves designed to avoid bringing United States nuclear power into play, we shall need better-equipped and highly mobile "conventional" forces. Some military experts contend that technological progress is taking us back to the World War I position when defensive weapons had a vast edge over offensive weapons. These men think that if we aim at a more balanced defense to deter attack—one scaled to the size of the aggression—the world's stability would be increased; we would not have to rely on potentially suicidal threats of massive retaliation (which some day might be called) to block a limited attack.

Obviously, a state of peace that depends upon a balance of terror is not a particularly happy or secure peace. It is going to get less secure year by year, as the nuclear weapons spread to n countries, including Communist China. The Russians will have to face up to the fact that the world is simply getting too dangerous for any of us.

But, as long as they are determined to beat or trick us into submission and the present kind of metastable peace is the best we can do—then, by gum, it's the best we can do. When they are ready to make genuine peace and settle down to live, we shall be ready, too.

That day had better come soon. For the research revolution has forced upon the world a new and breath-taking choice: lasting peace among the nations—or the peace of the grave.

9

A New Way to Grow

Held in check on the military front by the balance of
terror, the Soviets have shifted their attack to the economic
front. Khrushchev has said, "We declare war. We will win
over the United States. The threat to the United States
is not the ICBM, but in the field of peaceful production."
He has boasted of overtaking the United States economy

by 1970; worried United States officials—including spokes-
men of the Central Intelligence Agency—concede that, at
present United States and Soviet growth rates, this could
happen in a few decades. Even after squeezing all the water
out of Russian statistics, most American experts grant that
the Soviet economy has been growing at an annual rate
of about 7 per cent, at least double our own.

The new Soviet Seven-Year Plan, which runs from 1959
through 1965, does in fact represent a serious challenge
to the economic supremacy of the West and to its political
position in the uncommitted, underdeveloped nations of
the world. It is bound to give the U.S.S.R. a larger weight
in world trade and increase Western fears about Soviet
dumping.

There is not as much reassurance as you might think
from the realization that, even if this new Seven-Year Plan
is fulfilled in 1965 and the United States grows no faster
than we have in recent years, Soviet GNP would still be
not much more than 50 per cent of ours. (Soviet GNP is
presently a bit more than 40 per cent of ours.) But it must
be remembered that, out of their smaller GNP, the Soviets
are already able to put together a modern military program
of dimensions approximately equal to ours—because they
are allocating roughly 20 per cent of GNP to military and
foreign policy purposes, while we are allocating less than
10 per cent of our GNP to those purposes. Klaus Knorr,[1]
of the Center of International Studies at Princeton, has

[1] K. Knorr, *Can We Accelerate American Economic Growth?* Public Affairs
Service Report, Princeton, N.J., 1959, p. 13.

calculated that, if the United States GNP should continue to grow at a 3 per cent rate and if 10 per cent of GNP is allocated to national security, while the U.S.S.R. continued to grow at a 7 per cent rate and to allocate 20 per cent of GNP to national security, our relative positions in a couple of decades would look like this:

	United States (Billions)	Soviet Russia (Billions)
1958:		
Gross national product	$440	$176
National security expenditures	44	35
1978:		
Gross national product	796	686
National security expenditures	80	137

Startling results like these leave little room for complacency about this growth race.

Washington planners take the Soviet economic push seriously; they know that the Soviet Union has a good chance of achieving its over-all goals—although there are bound to be some shortfalls. In the past, the Russians have substantially fulfilled their Five-Year Plan goals. The sole exception was Khrushchev's 1956 Five-Year Plan, which was abandoned one year after it began.

The narrowing gap in economic strength between the United States and the U.S.S.R. will almost certainly make the Soviets much harder to deal with, both militarily and politically. The spectacle of the U.S.S.R. pulling up economically on the United States will have a psychological effect in underdeveloped countries; on top of that, more Soviet resources will become available for economic aid to underdeveloped countries, and for all the other military and scientific programs that lie at the heart of the twentieth-century power struggle.

To be sure, there has been a measure of nonsense spoken about this Soviet-American growth race. We are not in a war of gross statistics; if we were, it would probably pay us to put Darrell Huff (author of *How to Lie With Statistics*) in charge of the National Income Division of the Department of Commerce and really concoct some figures that would make heads spin in the underdeveloped countries.

Use of resources

Obviously, the way we use our resources is even more important than either the aggregate volume or the rate of growth of GNP. If the United States were simply to turn out more and more comic books, horror movies, and gin (all of which figure in GNP) while the Soviets put more and more of their growing GNP into science, technology, and integrated steel mills packaged for export, the United States would come out second best—or kaput—no matter what the GNP comparisons showed, and long before the Soviets drew abreast of us in GNP.

My friend Herb Stein of the CED has a wisecrack that I love; it goes, "If the Soviets can give us such a bad time when their GNP is less than half of ours, think what we can do to them when *our* GNP is half as big as theirs."

Take the effective way the Soviets have extracted political profit from their foreign-aid programs, which, through the 1950s, were still considerably smaller than ours. Most people got the idea that Soviet programs of aid to the underdeveloped countries were very large—that the Russians were prepared to pour out supplies of materials and machinery up to the limit that the underdeveloped countries were willing to take, given their concerns about political strings to Soviet aid or the damage they might do to their relations with the United States. The Soviets added to this impression by their lavish offers of aid to countries even within the Western camp, knowing that the great bulk of their offers would not be accepted.

The Soviets succeeded in creating the impression that the bulk of what they were sending to the underdeveloped countries was modern capital equipment and machinery. In fact, the Soviet Union was still a net importer of machinery. Most of the machinery and equipment going out under Soviet-bloc aid programs was actually coming from the East European satellites. Soviet aid projects usually involved building storage tanks, grain silos, roads, power dams, airfields—but rarely the equipping of large factories with lots of machinery. An important exception to this was the steel mill the Russians built for India at Bhilai—which the world took as typical of Soviet economic-aid programs.

In that Bhilai project the Soviets showed how adroitly they could combine economic aid, psychology, human relations. When I visited Bhilai in 1957, I learned from my Indian hosts that the Soviet engineers who built that mill refrained from consuming alcohol, because Bhilai is in a dry province. Such self-control is virtually unheard of among Americans—or Britishers and other Europeans —working at an overseas construction project. At Bhilai every Soviet engineer and technician worked side by side with the Indian who was to take over his job when the Russians had completed their work. This made a terrific impression on the Indians.

In their aid programs, as Hans Heymann of RAND has emphasized, the Russians have also shown a flair for public relations through such clever sales gimmicks as low interest rates, extended and easy terms of repayment, willingness to help dispose of local agricultural surpluses, dramatic visits at the top level, speedy economic agreements reached in a blaze of publicity, avoidance of protracted negotiations.

The Russians have been skilled symbol manipulators in their aid programs. They have put heavier and heavier emphasis on their scientific and technological accomplishments. They have set up a nuclear physics research laboratory in Cairo, an experimental atomic reactor in Belgrade, a technological institute in Rangoon. This emphasis on science and technology has helped to create the impression in the underdeveloped countries—and in some of the developed countries too—that the Soviet Union has not only caught up with the United States already but is rapidly plunging ahead of us. That, of course, is one of the great aims of their strategy: to convince the world that the wave of the future lies with them—that they are the once-poor nation that made good overnight—that other poor nations would do well to align themselves with the Soviets and follow their pattern of development. Big Brother is waiting to help you.

Growth and competitive coexistence

If they have done this well on slim resources (if we may proceed to forget Herb Stein's joke), what will they do when their resources are far more ample? Already their growing volume of economic aid to the underdeveloped countries is approaching the $1 billion mark—just about as much as we are giving to the poor countries.[2]

The mistake committed by those who deemphasize the importance of the economic competition between the United States and the Soviet Union, it seems to me, is that they regard the economic challenge in isolation from the total Communist political-military-psychological strategy for revolution, of which this economic offensive is a crucial part. If we floundered and failed on the economic front, while they forged ahead, year after year, the world would come to accept the Communists' ardently pro-

[2] Raymond Vernon, " 'Coexistence'? and 'Peaceful'?" *The New York Times Magazine,* July 10, 1960, p. 10.

moted image of old, decadent, dying capitalism and young, emergent, triumphant Communism as historical fact; and so it might become, particularly if we ever fell into another long period of stagnation, like the 1930s.

Growth is as important to the United States as it is to the Soviet Union as a means of making more resources available for national purposes. This is a point that needs to be made honestly and carefully, lest it smell of the kind of patriotism that is the last (or first) resort of scoundrels. Certainly, if we needed more resources for national security immediately, we could always get them by raising taxes; the United States can and must afford whatever is essential for national defense. Quite obviously, our opponent is economically far smaller than we and will be for a long time; hence, it's impossible for us to plead poverty if we fail to respond to his threats. As we have seen, the United States is currently spending less than 10 per cent of GNP on national security. During the Korean War (which we fought with no appreciable inconvenience to the home economy, although the public insisted on doing a certain amount of scare buying) national-security spending ran at about 13.5 per cent of GNP. During World War II, national defense took 27 per cent of GNP. The notion that there is some magic number beyond which defense spending may not go is nonsense. In any case, we are nowhere near that limit now. Obviously we shouldn't spend on defense—or anything else—just for the sake of spending; but no program essential to our nation's security need be foregone for budgetary reasons.

National tasks

Nevertheless, the fact remains that we are in this struggle for what is likely to be a very long pull. And it seems perfectly plain that economic growth is an incomparably better way than continuously increasing the tax burden to meet rising national requirements. Every competent group that has studied the trend of government expenditures in this country—and such studies have been done by or for the Gaither Committee, the Rockefeller Brothers Fund, the National Planning Association, the Committee for Economic Development—has concluded that the cost of government will continue to climb in the decade ahead, because of the threat to the nation from the Communists, the revolution of "rising expectations" in the underdeveloped countries, the pressure of growing population on public facilities, the changes in the age distribution of our population. Detailed study of national needs for defense, space research and exploration, foreign aid, atomic energy, highways, aviation, urban renewal, education, etc., has suggested that the total cash outlays of government—Federal, state and local—which in 1960 came to approximately $135 billion, may in 1970 come to something in the neighborhood of $200 billion.[3] We can meet such government

[3] Lest anyone think that a projected increase in total government spending to $200 billion by 1970 is improbable, consider what happened to government expenditures in the past decade. In 1950, the Department of Defense spent $12 billion; in 1960, $41 billion. In 1950, total Federal cash expenditures were $43 billion; in 1960, $95 billion. In 1950, total government (state, local, and Federal) cash payments were $62 billion; in 1960, $135 billion.

bills, without adding to our present tax burdens in relation to national income, if we maintain an average rate of growth of 4 to 5 per cent a year; and at the same time we can improve our standard of living. If we were to try to meet such levels of government expenditure as are projected for the decade ahead with lesser rates of growth, our tax burdens would mount, and our living standards would decline, accordingly. What would be more likely to happen is that we would simply not fulfill these projected government programs—and suffer whatever consequences to the national security or well-being that failure might imply.

Whether any of the existing studies of government-spending trends and national-growth requirements have adequately dealt with these longer-range problems or not, they have served the valuable purpose of focusing our attention on the right questions: What are the jobs the United States must do in the years ahead to solve pressing international and domestic problems? How much will those jobs cost? Would strong and sustained economic growth make it easier for the United States to do those jobs? What rate of growth for the United States economy is feasible—and how can we attain it? Those are the critical questions for today—and for the years to come; for growth has emerged as the paramount economic issue before the nation.

Summing up

In this book I have argued that the United States must grow—or prepare to endure some painful consequences. Population increase must be absorbed; jobs must be created for the rapidly growing labor force; the aspirations of the American people for higher living standards must be accommodated, if social tensions are to be resolved without government dictation; and the Communists' bid for world domination must be turned back.

Most of the debate over economic growth thus far has expended itself, just juggling numbers in rather superficial argument about the statistical race between the United States and the Russians—or between the Democrats and the Republicans. But economic growth involves much more than the year-to-year changes in production. Fundamentally, economic growth means growth in a nation's underlying ideas and skills. The immediate generator of economic growth is investment, whose fluctuations are certainly affected by many economic factors, such as levels of sales, capacity, profits, and the tax structure; but, more basically, investment arises from new ideas, new developments in science and technology, from education, research, innovations—new products, new processes, new resources; all these are the real seeds of long-term economic growth. Without the force of expanding technology, to generate investment, the mere act of saving would make little sense. Put most simply and crudely, why should Robinson Crusoe hoard coconuts, if he uses the free time left from producing his consumer goods just to sprawl on the beach? If he wants to improve his level of living, he must have some way to pour his saved-up free time into new technology— into making a canoe, or a plough, which will expand the productive capabilities of his island economy.

To be sure, Crusoe would not have to invent the canoe.

Similarly, "backward" nations can perhaps take technology for granted; they have to grow a long way to use up all the superior technologies available to them. But a highly developed country like the United States is not in that position; our growth depends essentially on improving technology.

One of the great advantages the Russians have had in the growth race up to now is that they have been able to pick up, ready-made, the superior technologies developed in the advanced capitalist countries. More and more, however, if they mean to catch and beat us, the Russians will have to show as much drive and imagination and originality in research and development all across the board as we have done; they will learn how much tougher the advance becomes when you have to push forward at the frontier. But we should not be complacent about their ability to do it; the Russians are well aware of the need to grow their own R&D and are pouring plenty of resources, men and material, into their effort.

We should be able to measure up to this Soviet challenge. Inventiveness and alertness to change are the very heart of the American character. More than a century ago, that most perceptive of tourists, Alexis de Tocqueville, wrote:

> I accost an American sailor and inquire why the ships of his country are built so as to last for only a short time; he answers without hesitation that the art of navigation is every day making such rapid progress that the finest vessel would become almost useless if it lasted beyond a few years. In these words, which fell accidentally, and on a

particular subject, from an uninstructed man, I recognize
the general and systematic idea upon which a great people
direct all their concerns.

More than ever before in our history, the American
people have in the postwar period acted upon this "general and systematic idea." We have fully come to understand that innovations need not be the accidental and
sporadic things they have been in the past. By a great new
emphasis on research, by systematizing innovation, industry and government now make regular provision for the
occurrence of new and unpredictable developments. This
process is just beginning. But already it is furnishing the
kind of spur to growth that came earlier from such individual developments as railroads or automobiles.

This research revolution seems to me to be a qualitative
change in the economy—one of the same importance to
future growth as the development of the concept of capital
investment itself was during the past two centuries.

Human capital

With this new growth force of systematized innovation,
there is no reason why the United States should not do even
better in the future than in the past. The coming together
in our time of new ideas in every field, new materials,
new tools of measurement and observation, new calculating
devices, new instruments of communication, new sources
of power, new information systems, new organizational
schemes—all this is producing the most powerful thrust
we have ever known.

Our problem is to harness that thrust—to use it to build up our national economic strength and to solve our international and domestic problems.

But the Soviets are trying to harness the same kind of thrust for their own purposes. Which holds the winning cards in such a competition—a free and democratic society like ours, or one that's controlled and directed from the top? We had better not be too smug or cocky in how we answer that question.

Theodore Schultz, the president of the American Economic Association, has stated the issue with dramatic clarity. In its investment in human resources and talents, he fears, the U.S.S.R. may be doing a better job than we are. Schultz says: "Herein lies the real possibility of the economy of the U.S.S.R. They are becoming exceedingly productive, despite the waste and inefficiency from their overcentralization. If I were to worry about the Russian economy—and I have seen it at first hand, and a good deal of it—it is in terms of the talents of the people that have risen—it is the creation of human capital that has taken place that is so extraordinary."

Do we, then, need to imitate the Russians? I think not— I certainly hope not. If this be patriotism, make the most of it, but I feel that the most powerful weapon in our hands, in our contest with them, is still our freedom, our respect for the rights and dignity of the individual, our commitment to the heritage of Western civilization and free political institutions. If we can prevent war, they must in time move in our direction. If they breed up a class of competent scientists and intellectuals, in the numbers they will require if they are to overtake us, they must give their people more freedom. And their people will wonder—as I think they have begun to wonder already, as I believe the whole Boris Pasternak affair demonstrated—where do we go from here? What was the revolution for? How about some peace and happiness? How about taking your damned foot off my neck?

The needed talents in our competition with the Communists aren't just scientific and technological. They must include imagination, drive, sympathy, organizing ability, insight and a feel for the way economic history is moving, energy, and courage—and all this among broad groups in the society.

This brings the study of growth around full circle to where it began centuries ago: The growth and power of nations depend primarily upon the qualities of their people.

That puts the focus of a long-term growth program not just on our tax laws, or on plant and equipment spending, but on our schools and colleges and universities and laboratories, and all the other seedbeds of American talent. We must do a better job of finding our most able people while they are young, developing their abilities, and providing employment and scope and challenge for their talents.

This certainly doesn't mean that every able or gifted

youngster should become a scientist or engineer; some of the talents we need most are those that can give meaning, direction, belief to our world.

A new experiment, a new setting of national goals and rebuilding of American institutions, is getting under way —confusedly, hesitantly, without full awareness of what's being tested or what the results will mean. If it succeeds, it will change the United States—and the world—as radically in the next half century as our world has changed from the quaint old world of 1910. The prospects opened up by the research revolution are exciting—and quite unpredictable.

10

A Program for Growth

When I had finished the first nine chapters of this book, I sent them off to Wassily Leontief and told him that I had decided not to end the book with a program for growth— a list of generalizations guaranteed to solve America's growth problem. Leontief replied: "Your decision not to try spelling out a program is quite right. As a matter of fact, an answer to the challenge we are facing is not so easy to find."

Leontief's own major conclusion, which he has stated in his introduction to this book, is startling and radical: Make all scientific and technological knowledge freely available to everyone. I think Leontief overstates himself. As I sought to show in Chapter 7, "Why Research Spending Soars," the quest for profits is, in our system, a powerful force for the discovery of new knowledge and new technology—and I believe that the process of discovery is even more crucial than the process of diffusion; for, as every military intelligence officer knows, all secrets are dated—knowledge will be diffused, willy-nilly. Indeed, the quest for profits is also a powerful force for accelerating diffusion, as well as for promoting discovery. I think Chapter 4 on semiconductors makes that crystal-clear.

This is not to say, however, that a part of the job of discovery and diffusion of scientific and technological knowledge should not be "socialized"; that is precisely what we are doing through government support of basic research—and of applied research in many critical areas— as well as through our publicly supported educational system. And I certainly do believe that we need to strengthen our public support for both research and education. Further, I suspect that we need a major re-examination of our patent and licensing laws to make sure that they are doing the best possible job of providing strong incentives for discovery without unduly arresting the diffusion of new technology. The antitrust laws must also be used to serve the same positive ends; remember that it was antitrust action that unlocked *Mother Bell's Cookbook* and pro-

duced the fantastic growth of the semiconductor industry
—which nourished the growth of other industries, too.

But I still believe that the worst thing I could do at this
point would be to provide a tight set of conclusions which
might shut off the reader's thought and imagination. My
own conclusions—where I firmly have them—can be found
in the preceding chapters. I hope the reader will plunge
back and try to make up his own mind about what needs
to be done, if the analysis of this book is valid.

APPENDIX

The Outlook for Expenditures on Research and Development during the Next Decade

Dexter M. Keezer, Douglas Greenwald,
and Robert P. Ulin

Our assignment on this occasion is to make a ten-year fore-cast of expenditures for scientific research and development in the United States.

In doing so, we shall use the concepts of scientific research and development devised by the National Science Foundation and employed in its surveys and studies of this range of activity. The concept of research and development, subsequently to be abbreviated as R and D, which the Foundation uses in its studies of industrial research and development "includes basic and applied research in the sciences (including medicine) and in engineering, and design and development of prototypes and processes. It does not include nontechnological activities and technical service, such as quality control, routine product testing, market research, sales promotion, sales service, geological or geophysical exploration, or research in the social sciences or

213

psychology." In its studies of *government* R and D and that of *non-profit institutions,* the Foundation includes in its concept· research in the social sciences.

Whether research in the social sciences is included or left out makes relatively little difference in the totals of expenditures for R and D. Social science research is only a small drop in the total R and D bucket. In a subversive way, this very disproportion may ultimately prove to be one of the most significant aspects of the total development of R and D. We have in mind, of course, the tremendous changes which scientific R and D is making in our physical environment without any balancing by systematic study of what it is doing to the human beings involved.

Both the National Science Foundation figures on the cost of R and D and our own figures cover many indirect costs, as well as the direct R and D costs. For example, service and supporting costs are included. Thus salaries of stenographers and file clerks assigned to R and D sections are part of the total. In addition, a reasonable share of overhead is also included. Thus administrative costs, space charges or rent and even depreciation on research buildings and equipment are part of the total R and D cost. However, our R and D figures include only those capital costs that are allocated to the current research effort (i.e. depreciation charges). They do not include the original capital expenditures for research buildings and equipment which are charged to capital account.

Our principal qualifications to carry out our forecasting assignment are probably these two:

1. For a number of years we have made annual surveys of the plans of business firms to make expenditures for R and D and the degree to which plans have been fulfilled.[1] These opera-

---

[1] Douglas Greenwald, "The Annual McGraw-Hill Research and Development Survey," *Methodology of Statistics on Research and Development,* National Science Foundation, Washington, D.C., 1959, pp. 53–55.

tions have given us some knowledge of the outlook for expenditures for R and D.

Our studies of plans and performance in the field of R and D were an outgrowth of our continuing studies and surveys in the field of business investment in new producing facilities. We recognized that what is done in the field of R and D has a major bearing on what will be done in the field of business investment in new producing facilities subsequently.

We also had no difficulty in seeing that what is going on and is in prospect in the field of R and D constitutes what is probably the most dramatic as well as the most dynamic aspect of the American economy today. It is a shame that, of themselves, the words research and development, are so static and uninspiring. For they tend to damp down and blur their true significance.

2. We are courageous enough, or, as many of you will feel, foolhardy enough to attempt a 10-year forecast of R and D.

When it comes to forecasting, we do not share the diffidence of most of our academic confreres. As we observe them, they concentrate primarily on what has been happening and is happening and shrink from forecasting until they think they know. This means that, as a practical matter, they do very little forecasting.

As business economists we must do forecasting. It is a key element of business planning. Also, we find that an attempt to make a forecast can be quite as good an analytical device and a better teaching device than an analysis concentrated on the historical record. In fact, an effort to forecast what will be the price of copper or coffee a year or two hence can be made to constitute not only a very good course in economics, but pretty much the whole of the social sciences. And it would be a course which has an obvious relevance which a backward looking course sometimes seems to lack.

We are fully aware, of course, of the great limitations of the materials with which we must work in making a forecast of R and D. The quality of the information about current expenditures for R and D leaves a geat deal to be desired. Also, for purposes of analysis and forecasting, the going concept of R and D is an extremely cumbersome instrument. As has been indicated, it covers not only operations of decidedly different character such as basic research and product development, but also operations which respond to quite different incentives and economic forces.

If there is a unifying element of the going concept of R and D it probably is that all of it, in one way and another, is directed to innovation of one kind or another. But much of the innovation involved is that attendant upon the cold war which means that the forecasting of it involves the appraisal of forces and attitudes as mysterious and remote as those stemming from Moscow and Peiping.

Happily there is work in progress on the forecasting of expenditures for R and D which will lead to at least a much more polished product, particularly in the area of industrial R and D, than we can make available today. Professor Yale Brozen of the Graduate School of Business of the University of Chicago, who, so far as we know, has been the leading pioneer in this field of inquiry, has in charge an impressive range of such work.[2]

In the meantime, no more than a rough and ready forecast of R and D expenditures for any period beyond the immediate future is possible. But, clearly labeled and recognized

[2] Yale Brozen, "The Economic Future of Research and Development," *Industrial Laboratories,* December, 1953; "Scientific Advance as a Factor in Economic Change," paper delivered at the Seventh Conference on Scientific Manpower, National Science Foundation, Washington, D.C., 1957; "The Future of Industrial Research," University of Chicago project, 1960.

as just that, a longer range forecast is, we believe, worth making.

We propose to deal with the subject of research and development under three broad headings: (1) a forecast of the probable increase in R and D expenditures over the next decade, (2) an analysis of the forces that are working to bring about this increase—particularly in the area of private business expenditures for R and D, and (3) a few summary comments on the implications of these trends in the growth of R and D expenditures for business and public policies.

A forecast of research and development expenditures

We have already noted that all forecasts of R and D expenditures must be given in terms of data that are admittedly shaky —both as to coverage and definition. Nevertheless, we shall proceed to a forecast in terms of quite specific numbers for 1959 and 1969, in order to give some quantitative significance to the trends we shall describe. This audience is well equipped to discriminate between exact and rough statistics, and we shall not belabor the point. What we are dealing with here are general orders of magnitude.

Our forecast of R and D expenditures is developed in the three tables following, showing expenditures on R and D (1) by major sources of funds, (2) by agencies performing the work and, (3) by type of research project—basic research, applied research or product development. Even if the forecasts embodied in these tables should by some mischance prove to be grossly misguided, the historical segment of the tables would still constitute a net addition (and we believe a net addition of substantial importance) to our knowledge of R and D expenditures. Indeed, it may be safely said that they constitute the best set of estimates of R and D expenditures running back to the year 1945 which is extant, because it is, as far as we know, the only set of such estimates. It is also a set of estimates which staff members of the National Science Foundation checked and could not improve upon. The estimates take into account data compiled by this Foundation, by the Defense Department, the Bureau of Labor Statistics, the Census Bureau, and our own Department of Economics.

In summary, as the figures in the tables indicate, we expect the total expenditure for R and D to increase from about $12 billion in 1959 to about $22 billion in 1969. This forecast is in terms of current dollars, which we estimate—conservatively —will reflect an increase of about $\frac{1}{4}$ in costs of research manpower and equipment. For the past decade . . . and presumably for the next decade . . . these costs have tended to increase considerably faster than the general price level. The corresponding 1969 figure in constant 1959 dollars would be about $17.5 billion.

The tables also indicate prospective shifts in the character of R and D spending. The prospect is that in 1969 a smaller share of the total will be devoted to government research (particularly defense-type) and larger shares relatively will be devoted to industrial research and to basic research generally than is the case now. Also, a decade hence the proportion of basic and applied research, as opposed to product development, promises to be increased. We would regard the reasons, now to be arrayed, as of much more abiding significance than any precise dimensions of the conclusions to be drawn at this juncture.

Expenditures and sources of funds

In addition to the availability of money and the incentives to apply it to R and D, there are numerous other factors which could have a key bearing on the future course of expenditures for this range of activity. While it is our impression that it will not prove a seriously limiting factor, one of them is the availability of enough competent scientists and engineers to staff the R and D establishment adequately.[3] Here, however, we limit our analysis primarily to the prospective availability of funds and the incentives to increase the flow of funds to R and D. In so doing, we lead off with the establishment which now provides the larger part of the grand total of funds for R and D—the federal government.

At the present time, the federal government is the main provider of funds: $7 billion in 1959, of which $6 billion is connected, in one way or another, with the defense program. (This includes expenditures by the Dept. of Defense and several other agencies, most notably the Atomic Energy Commission). Most of the increase in R and D spending during the past two

[3] In the McGraw-Hill survey taken in the spring of 1957, manufacturing companies were asked questions about future needs for scientists and engineers in research and development work. At that time they expected to employ 15% more scientists and engineers in R and D over the three year period 1958–1960. This need for scientific manpower was tied to a planned increase in R and D expenditures of 27%. This means that for every 9% increase in R and D spending, a 5% increase in scientific manpower is needed. On this basis we would need about 45% more scientists and engineers in R and D in 1969 than we have today. R and D employment objectives obviously are high and will require a relatively high number of scientific and engineering graduates in the future. But if the total number of these graduates continues to increase, as we expect, it should not be difficult to supply R and D with scientific manpower. The flexibility of the supply of technical manpower is remarkable, even over short periods of time. A recent study for the National Science Foundation by the Bureau of Labor Statistics indicates that between January, 1954 and January, 1957—a period during which there were about 70,000 bachelors' degrees awarded in Engineering—employment of engineers in industry alone rose by over 100,000. It seems clear that many persons without formal degrees can be trained to do routine technical work and that many engineers can be released either from such routine functions or from various non-engineering jobs to which they have drifted in slacker times. (*Science and Engineering in American Industry,* National Science Foundation, 1957.)

decades has resulted from the willingness, or—if you like—the compulsion of Congress to appropriate funds for R and D connected with national defense.

It does not seem irresponsible to suggest that in 1959, and looking forward to the 1960's pressures of this sort have begun to slacken just a bit. Whatever one's personal view of Mr. Khrushchev and his ideas on coexistence, there seems to have been enough relaxation of international tensions to abate some of the enthusiasm for rapid increases in defense spending that accompanied the first *sputnik*. The federal budget for fiscal 1961 does not include, according to preliminary reports, any increase in defense spending. And there is some reason to believe that such increases as may occur thereafter will be of limited proportions. This is not only because of the changing climate of international relations, which may permit a slowing down in the arms race, but also—and perhaps more important —because the Department of Defense has developed, in recent years, an increasingly effective set of budgetary controls—so that any future step-up in defense requirements will be accompanied by a better selection of projects and a less wasteful expansion of expenditures than occurred in the 1950s.

Considered in this context, what is likely to be the course of R and D expenditures in the defense sector? Even if spending on production of weapons is reduced or held relatively constant, spending for R and D is likely to go on increasing because (1) whatever armaments we do produce will be more complex, in a scientific sense, and (2) any reduction in key armaments programs would probably mean a shift of some resources to semi-civilian projects, such as those of the National Aeronautics and Space Agency, that have some longer-range utility from a defense standpoint. In fact, a good theoretical case can be made that such a shift would accelerate R and D spending. Some of the detection and warning devices required to police an effective disarmament scheme would require more extensive R and D than the weapons they are supposed to detect.

However, as a practical matter, civilian administrators—in research, or anything else—are always less wasteful than the military. And in fact, the very nature of military problems compels some duplicating programs that would not be undertaken in a more rational world. Consequently, we expect that defense-type R and D expenditures will increase at a slower rate during the next decade than it has in recent years.

A specific forecast can be no more than an intelligent guess, but our guess is an increase of $4 billion from 1959 to 1969, or less than a half-billion per year. Considering the facts that in the past five years the *total* defense budget has only increased about $1 billion per year (and the entire federal budget less than $3 billion per year), we might reasonably conclude that $400 million a year would not be regarded as a niggardly increase in R and D spending for defense projects. The amount would undoubtedly be raised during any renewal of near-hostilities, but as noted above, improved budgetary controls would limit the rise better than was the case after Korea.

Turning to other types of R and D financed by the government, we find that these include research in such fields as medicine, agriculture, and the support of educational institutions engaged in pure science. In fact, the bulk of them could be grouped either under "Agriculture" or under "Health, Education, and Welfare," to use the cabinet titles. In other words, these are expenditures that, at least indirectly, provide continuing benefit for certain groups of Congressional constituents—as opposed to expenditures by the Dept. of Defense, whose products go up in smoke (when they do go up) at Cape Canaveral.

The Congress seems to have a more consistently generous attitude toward such expenditures than it does toward the Defense program. Non-defense research expenditures, financed by the federal government, have doubled in the past two years, and there is no reason why this trend should not continue. In fact, certain new developments may reinforce the trend: (1) "Research" has become a popular label for civilian expenditure programs. It no longer connotes long-haired professors doing useless experiments, but products of real value to business, agriculture, community health and education. It is a label that helps to pass appropriations. (2) The National Science Foundation has lately become an effective (almost cabinet-level) spokesman on the need for such expenditures and has collected data that give Congress a clear picture of the total R and D spending included in the federal budget. In view of the widely advertised competition with Soviet Russia, it seems likely that Congress will want to keep the total U.S. effort moving ahead at a fair clip, and any decline in defense-sponsored R and D will encourage increases in non-defense projects, which do not lack for sponsors.

In this sector, as in the defense sector, our forecast must be highly conjectural, because it depends on political considerations. But a doubling of the (much smaller) total of nondefense federal research spending in ten years seems like a conservative bet.

After considering government-financed R and D expenditures, we find that the remaining expenditures are financed almost entirely by private industry, which this year is spending $4.5 billion, with only a very small part—$300 million—financed by universities, research foundations and other non-profit institutions. Industrial research and development is a field we know considerably more about, as to motivations and prospects, than we do about the future of government R and D. Our knowledge is primarily the result of surveys conducted by the National Science Foundation, the McGraw-Hill Department of Economics and investigators at a number of universities.[4] These studies give considerable depth to our knowledge of private R and D expenditures during the past ten years, and the latest McGraw-Hill survey reports industry's plans ahead to 1962.

On the basis of the trends so laid out, we can forecast, with some confidence, that private industry's expenditures will continue to increase rapidly, at least doubling by 1969 and perhaps increasing even more. The expenditures financed by non-profit institutions will show an even more rapid rate of growth percentage-wise (although remaining small in absolute terms) because (1) they are starting up from a relatively low level and (2) the increasing public awareness of the need for scientific research has speeded up the flow of contributions (including business contributions) to these non-profit institutions...so that spending can now rise sharply.

If we summarize the effects of these shifts in financing, we can see that they produce a shift in the purpose of research programs. We find that expenditures on defense-connected R and D will show less than average growth over the next decade. R and D aimed at making a profit, research simply to advance knowledge, and research to attain social and cultural objectives will grow relatively fast.

We translate our forecast of the availability of R and D funds into R and D performance in Table 2. Whereas government has been and will continue to be the biggest provider of R and D money, industry has been and will continue to be the main performer of R and D. It is noteworthy, however, that colleges and other institutions will increase their share of R and D performance over the next decade.

[4] See Raymond H. Ewell, "The Role of Research in Economic Growth," *Chemical and Engineering News,* July 18, 1955, p. 2980.

We also find a shift in the types of individual research products to be undertaken. At the present time (see Table 3), "research and development" is overwhelmingly "development," i.e., the design and development of specific new products from the results of previous research. This kind of activity accounts for most of the military research and development program, and most of the private expenditures as well. Only $3.6 billion, out of the $12 billion spent on research and development in 1959, is for research in the laboratory sense—basic and applied research. And this is concentrated in a relatively few industries (aircraft, electronics, machinery and electrical equipment) and, so far as basic research is concerned, in government and university laboratories.

By 1969, we may expect a rather substantial shift. Product development will still be the predominant type of project, but basic and applied research will increase to 41% of the average research dollar, compared to 30% in 1959. The shift will result mainly from less emphasis on defense work (more on basic science) in the government sector, and partly from a trend toward complex R and D (as opposed to mere gadgetry) in industry.

The purpose of research in industry

We now turn to a discussion of the factors that have a special importance in the continuing rapid growth of private industry's expenditures on research and development. Clearly this has been a growing activity—we might almost say a "growth industry"—over the past decade. Private expenditures on R and D have increased from $1.4 billion in 1949 to $4.5 billion in 1959, or by 220% in 10 years. What has caused this tripling of expenditures?

Some of the original impetus undoubtedly came from wartime efforts in research and development, which demonstrated the feasibility of organizing for this work on a large scale and scheduling whole projects from applied research through the development of finished products—whereas in peacetime, most business firms had not made much connection between original research and product marketing. Moreover, the wartime R and D created a considerable backlog of knowledge that could be applied to the development of peacetime products. Some companies with long-established research programs—particularly in the chemical and electrical industries—had a further backlog of prewar applied research that they found profitable to develop in the expanding postwar markets. All of these factors helped to swell R and D spending during 1947–1953, but this early postwar boom was concentrated in the few industries that had extensive prewar or wartime research experience—chemicals, electrical, aircraft, electronics and a few sections of the machinery industry.

The annual returns on investment, for R and D performed in these industries, were extremely high—in some cases amounting to several dollars for each research dollar invested. For example, in 1951 one large oil company reported a total return of $15.40 for each research dollar invested, and a large paper company, a return of $10 per year on each research dollar.[5]

As these facts began to attract attention, firms in other industries began to mark larger R and D investments. From 1954 on, the increase outside the traditional "research-based" industries has been particularly rapid. Financial incentives were increased by a 1954 revision in the tax law, which permitted R and D expenditures to be deducted as a current expense, instead of treated as a capital investment for tax purposes. But the most important factor was probably the return of vigorous competition to postwar markets, after the end of the Korean

[5] Allan Abrams, "Measuring the Return from Research," *Proceedings of the Fourth Annual Conference on the Administration of Research,* University of Michigan, Ann Arbor, Mich., 1951.

hostilities. In the past five years, more and more companies have turned to R and D as a competitive weapon, enabling them to offer new or improved products, and to reduce the costs of manufacturing by new processes that save labor or materials.

A McGraw-Hill survey in 1958 reported fairly complete data on why companies were increasing their R and D programs. In answer to the question: "What will be the main purpose of your research program?", 41% of the responding manufacturing firms specified "improvement in present products." Another 48% specified "new products," and 11% specified "new processes." These answers emphasize the very great preponderance of development in total "research and development" outlays. Improvements to existing products clearly do not require much fundamental—or even much applied—research, and a large proportion of the outlays on new products occurs in industries, such as food or automobiles, where the proportion of research on such products is small relative to development. Because of the large backlog of applied research information that has been available (primarily from the efforts of a relatively few large companies), the majority of firms have been able to concentrate on the highly profitable business of product and process development.

These programs to develop new or improved products generally yield quick returns, as indicated by manufacturing companies' replies to another question in the same survey: "How soon do you expect your expenditures on research and development to pay off?" Fully 39% of the respondents expected a payoff in less than three years (which corresponds closely with the 41% concentrating on the improvement of present products —the quickest payoff type of project). Another 52% expected a payoff in three to five years (corresponding roughly to the 59% developing new products or processes—but obviously omitting some of those projects that required really difficult research and development). Only 9% put the payoff period at six years or more, which may be taken as a rough indication of the proportion of firms (even large firms which constituted much of the sample) engaged in really fundamental research.

These rates of return on research were (and continue to be) significantly better than the typical return, or "payoff," on investment in new plant and equipment. In 1955, (when expectations as to rate of return were undoubtedly higher for plant and equipment than in 1958) the McGraw-Hill survey found that 17% of manufacturing firms expected new equipment to pay off in three years or less (compared to 39% for investment in research); 64% had a three to five year payoff period (compared to 52%); and 19% figured six years or more (compared to 9%). These comparisons make it clear why many companies with a given amount of capital to reinvest found it profitable to increase the proportion going to research and development. The generally rising level of corporate cash flow, the deductibility of research expenditures for tax purposes, and the availability of a relatively large fund of scientific knowledge that had not been exploited commercially were all contributing factors.

In addition, the research boom—once it got started—tended to feed on itself. Because of the competitive factor, each increase in research outlays bred more increases. The development of new engines in the automobile and aircraft industries required the development of new fuels by the oil companies who wanted the new business. Substitution of aluminum for steel, plastics for wood, synthetic fibers for older textiles—all have led to more research in the industries affected, either to fight off the substitutes by improving product quality, or to develop new uses for the old products. This inter-product and inter-industry competition is still going on furiously, and promises to be a continuing spur to R and D. Rates of return are still high enough to stimulate ventures into new products and processes. And where these projects succeed, they are bound to provoke additional research and development programs as a counter-reaction by firms seeking to maintain their shares of the market.

This brings us up to 1959, with the forces behind the research boom still strong. But are they strong enough to bring about another tripling of research expenditures in the decade ahead? In our judgment they are not. Industrial research is still a "growth industry," but as in other such cases, the *rate* of growth is likely to slow down somewhat as this industry matures. During the last ten years—with the stimulus of high returns—industrial research has at least half-way grown up to its near-term potential. There is still a fairly large amount of fundamental scientific knowledge that has not been exploited commercially, but this backlog has been reduced considerably since the end of World War II. Much of the older applied research has been carried through to product development, and much of our store of basic science is being utilized, by one firm or another, in current applied research projects. This is especially so in the industries—like chemicals and electrical equipment—where the science base was established prewar. Other industries are further behind in exploiting their science base, or in doing the basic research needed to create such a base. But it is hard to think of an industry today where at least a start has not been made on exploiting the immediate research potential.

From now on increases in the expenditures for product development will require more proportionate increases in applied research than was the case some years ago. And inevitably, the growth of applied research will require—sooner or later—an expansion of our base in fundamental science. All this can be done. Industry is already shifting more toward a heavier pro-

portion of applied and basic research, and we have included
these shifts in our forecast for 1969, as previously given. However, such shifts are bound to slow down the overall growth
of R and D expenditures for two reasons: (1) as noted above,
the more laborious types of research do not pay off as quickly,
and funds for such projects will be harder to get (2) basic and
applied research require highly trained scientists and engineers
—not merely technicians—and the supply of such people is
relatively limited. It is increasing, to be sure,—as we noted
previously—and so research and development expenditures will
continue to increase, but not as fast as when there was a large
backlog of research to be quickly converted into new products
by engineering talent.

Finally, there is the matter of profitability. The average rate
of return on research and development has been well above the
return on investment in plant and equipment during the past
decade. It seems likely to remain higher for at least the next
five years, but as competition in research and in new products
increases, the differential is bound to narrow. By 1965, new
equipment may be almost as good a bet in many cases. Furthermore, the whole economy will be changing by 1965 because we
shall be entering a period of very rapid growth in the number
of new families and rapid growth in most consumer markets—
a period, therefore, that is likely to offer increasingly good returns on the expansion of plant capacity. In this new atmosphere, the incentives to increase R and D programs will still be
strong for most companies, because labor and materials will
still be costly and research points out ways to save them. All
we have done in the preceding discussion is to indicate why we
think it is reasonable to figure that R and D spending by industry will about double in the next decade, instead of tripling
as in the past decade.

Implications for policy

If research expenditures are estimated to double in the next ten years, there would appear little need for public concern about the quantity of research we get. In absolute terms, it will be enormous—perhaps as great as can be absorbed by our facilities for introducing new production processes and marketing new products. In our Department of Economics, we have estimated that as much as 20% of all the products to be marketed in 1969 will be items that are not on the market today. This is perhaps as high a proportion as it would be practical to attempt, considering the concentration of effort that is required to introduce and market new products successfully. There are similar limits to the number of new things that can be tried out on production lines, although in the long-run the economy would be well served by innovations that permit mass production with a smaller capital investment. Research in this direction may increase faster than new product research as we get into the mid-1960s.

In any event, incentives for applied research and product development are very strong, and likely to remain so without further changes in public policy. We will get a large enough quantity of new products and processes.[6] There may, however, be reason to worry about the quality of our research effort, in the sense that there are insufficient incentives for basic research. Our own surveys indicate that most industrial companies do not do that kind of research because it takes too long to pay off. Other studies have indicated that too much of the government's research effort (and too many of its grants to universities) is concentrated on applied research, and too little on

[6] Robert P. Ulin, "What Will Research Bring About?" *Thinking Ahead, Harvard Business Review,* January–February, 1958.

basic research, if the latter is to receive the impetus it needs from government sources.

It is possible that industry could be persuaded to undertake more basic research by specific tax incentives—say a doubling of the normal deduction. It might also be persuaded (although this seems less effective) by a simple reduction in corporate tax rates—which would shorten payout periods on all types of investment. Some companies engaged in defense work say that they would do more basic research, if they were allowed a bigger profit on defense contracts. And presumably straight subsidies could be employed to encourage companies with large applied research programs to do more basic work.

However, it seems to us that there are serious limitations on any incentive scheme designed to get more basic research done in industry. The trouble is that most industrial companies cannot use the results of such research. By definition, basic research does not have a specific product or market objective; there is no telling what it will turn up. Very few companies have such broad production or marketing facilities that they can use whatever is discovered, and very few have the capital to wait out the long periods of basic research plus applied research before they get to product development.[7] The burden falls back on a few large companies (most of them defense contractors), the universities and the government.

This is true in spite of the fact that, in companies which actually do basic research, the association with basic scientists seems to improve the work of the applied research staff and lead to a higher percentage of success in applied research projects. Some research directors believe, therefore, that up to 10% or even 15% of a total R and D budget can *profitably* be

[7] Richard R. Nelson, "The Simple Economics of Basic Scientific Research," *The Journal of Political Economy*, University of Chicago Press, Chicago, June, 1959.

allocated to basic research, simply on the basis of the resulting improvement in work of the entire staff.[8] This educational and training value may lead to somewhat more basic research in industry during the next decade, but we must assume that the number of companies involved will continue to be relatively limited.

Therefore, an indiscriminate program to encourage basic research would probably not succeed. It would seem more practical to concentrate any incentive or subsidy program on the limited group of companies described above, on the efforts of some government agencies—and particularly on the universities, which have the ideal climate for basic research. When we look at the important discoveries in basic science that have come from our universities, and then look at the small size of the expenditures in their sector, it is difficult to avoid the conclusion that the nation would derive enormous long-run benefits from an increase—proportionately a very large increase—in this area of research. In our forecast of R and D spending for 1969, we have assumed that appropriate steps would be taken in this direction, but we would be delighted to find, ten years hence, that we underestimated the American people's willingness to support the pursuit of fundamental knowledge.

[8] Based on preliminary results of a University of Chicago study directed by Prof. Yale Brozen.

APPENDIX TABLES

Table 1. Research and Development Estimates: Major Sources of Funds

Year	In billions of dollars		Government				Colleges and institutions	Percentage of total		
	Total	Industry	Total	Industry	To government labs	To colleges and institutions		Industry	Government	Colleges and other institutions
1945	$1.8	$0.9	$0.8	$0.3	$0.4	$0.1	$.1	50	44	6
1946	2.1	1.0	1.0	0.4	0.4	0.2	.1	48	48	4
1947	2.7	1.3	1.3	0.6	0.5	0.2	.1	48	48	4
1948	3.1	1.4	1.6	0.8	0.6	0.2	.1	45	52	3
1949	3.1	1.4	1.6	0.8	0.6	0.2	.1	45	52	3
1950	3.4	1.5	1.8	0.9	0.7	0.2	.1	44	53	3
1951	4.0	1.8	2.0	1.0	0.8	0.2	.2	45	50	5
1952	4.5	2.0	2.3	1.1	0.9	0.3	.2	44	51	5
1953	4.9	2.2	2.5	1.2	1.0	0.3	.2	45	51	4
1954	5.5	2.4	2.8	1.4	1.1	0.3	.3	44	51	5
1955	6.3	2.5	3.5	1.8	1.2	0.5	.3	40	56	4
1956	8.4	2.9	5.2	3.1	1.4	0.7	.3	37	60	3
1957	10.0	3.5	6.2	3.7	1.6	0.9	.3	35	62	3
1958	11.0	4.0	6.7	4.1	1.6	1.0	.3	36	61	3
1959	12.0	4.5	7.2	4.6	1.6	1.0	.3	37	60	3
1969	22.2	9.0	12.4	7.5	2.4	2.5	.8	40	56	4

Table 2. Research and Development Estimates: Agencies Performing the Work

	Billions of dollars				Percentages of total		
Year	Total	In-dustry	Govern-ment	Colleges and in-stitutions	In-dustry	Govern-ment	Colleges and in-stitutions
1945	$1.8	$1.2	$0.4	$0.2	67	22	11
1946	2.1	1.4	0.4	0.3	67	19	14
1947	2.7	1.9	0.5	0.3	70	19	11
1948	3.1	2.2	0.6	0.3	71	19	10
1949	3.1	2.2	0.6	0.3	71	19	10
1950	3.4	2.4	0.7	0.3	71	20	9
1951	4.0	2.8	0.8	0.4	70	20	10
1952	4.5	3.1	0.9	0.5	69	20	11
1953	4.9	3.4	1.0	0.5	69	21	10
1954	5.5	3.8	1.1	0.6	69	20	11
1955	6.3	4.3	1.2	0.8	68	19	13
1956	8.4	6.0	1.4	1.0	71	17	12
1957	10.0	7.2	1.6	1.2	72	16	12
1958	11.0	8.1	1.6	1.3	74	14	12
1959	12.0	9.1	1.6	1.3	76	13	11
1969	22.2	16.5	2.4	3.3	74	11	15

Table 3. Research and Development Estimates: Types of Research Projects

(In billions of dollars)

Year	Total	Total — Basic		Total — Applied		Total — Development		Industry Total	Industry — Basic		Industry — Applied		Industry — Development	
1945	$1.8	$0.18	10%	$0.44	24%	$1.18	66%	$1.2	$.05	4%	$0.24	20%	$0.91	76%
1946	2.1	0.24	11	0.52	25	1.34	64	1.4	.06	4	0.28	20	1.06	76
1947	2.7	0.26	10	0.65	24	1.79	66	1.9	.08	4	0.38	20	1.44	76
1948	3.1	0.28	9	0.74	24	2.08	67	2.2	.09	4	0.44	20	1.67	76
1949	3.1	0.28	9	0.74	24	2.08	67	2.2	.09	4	0.44	20	1.67	76
1950	3.4	0.30	9	0.80	24	2.30	67	2.4	.10	4	0.48	20	1.82	76
1951	4.0	0.35	9	0.95	24	2.70	67	2.8	.11	4	0.56	20	2.13	76
1952	4.5	0.42	9	1.08	24	3.00	67	3.1	.12	4	0.62	20	2.36	76
1953	4.9	0.43	9	1.15	23	3.32	68	3.4	.12	3.5	0.66	19.5	2.62	77
1954	5.5	0.49	9	1.30	24	3.71	67	3.8	.13	3.5	0.74	19.5	2.93	77
1955	6.3	0.59	9	1.49	24	4.22	67	4.3	.14	3.5	0.84	19.5	3.82	77
1956	8.4	0.76	9	1.96	23	5.68	68	6.0	.21	3.5	1.17	19.5	4.62	77
1957	10.0	0.89	9	2.33	23	6.78	68	7.2	.24	3.5	1.40	19.5	5.56	77
1958	11.0	0.93	8	2.51	23	7.56	69	8.1	.24	3.0	1.54	19.0	6.32	78
1959	12.0	0.96	8	2.68	22	8.36	70	9.1	.27	3.0	1.73	19.0	7.10	78
1969	22.2	2.84	13	6.28	28	13.08	59	16.5	.83	5	4.12	25.0	11.55	70

Year	Government							Colleges and other institutions						
	Total	Basic		Applied		Development		Total	Basic		Applied		Development	
1945	$0.4	$.03	8%	$.12	30%	$0.25	62%	$0.2	$0.10	50%	$0.08	40%	$.02	10%
1946	0.4	.03	8	.12	30	0.25	62	0.3	0.15	49	0.12	40	.03	11
1947	0.5	.04	8	.15	30	0.31	62	0.3	0.14	48	0.12	40	.04	12
1948	0.6	.05	8	.18	30	0.37	62	0.3	0.14	48	0.12	40	.04	12
1949	0.6	.05	8	.18	30	0.37	62	0.3	0.14	47	0.12	40	.04	13
1950	0.7	.06	8	.20	29	0.44	63	0.3	0.14	47	0.12	40	.04	13
1951	0.8	.06	8	.23	29	0.51	63	0.4	0.18	46	0.16	40	.06	14
1952	0.9	.07	8	.26	29	0.57	63	0.5	0.23	46	0.20	40	.07	14
1953	1.0	.08	8	.29	29	0.63	63	0.5	0.23	45	0.20	40	.07	15
1954	1.1	.09	8	.32	29	0.69	63	0.6	0.27	45	0.24	40	.09	15
1955	1.2	.10	8	.33	28	0.77	64	0.8	0.35	44	0.32	40	.13	16
1956	1.4	.11	8	.39	28	0.90	64	1.0	0.44	44	0.40	40	.16	16
1957	1.6	.13	8	.45	28	1.02	64	1.2	0.52	43	0.48	40	.20	17
1958	1.6	.13	8	.45	28	1.02	64	1.3	0.56	43	0.52	40	.22	17
1959	1.6	.13	8	.43	27	1.04	65	1.3	0.56	43	0.52	40	.22	17
1969	2.4	.36	15	.84	35	1.20	50	3.3	1.65	50	1.32	40	.33	10

Index

Abramovitz, Moses, 31
Abrams, Allan, 225
Accelerator theories of investment, 131
Aerojet-General Corporation, 177
AFL-CIO, 124
Africa, 13, 14, 150
Agricultural research, 7, 221
Air Force, U.S., 66, 106
Air Reduction Company, Inc., 108
American Economic Association, 206
American Telephone & Telegraph Company, 75, 76, 175–177
Amperex Electronic Corporation, 91
Anderson, A. E., 84, 85
Army, U.S., 94, 123
Asia, 13, 14, 150
Atlas missile, 189
Atomic bomb, 55, 181, 183
Atomic Energy Commission, 219
Auden, W. H., 102

Bakalar, David, 98
Bakalar, Leo, 98
Balance of payments, 12, 144
Bardeen, John, 71
Baxter Laboratories, Inc., 177
Belgium, 41
Belgrade, 198
Bell, Alexander Graham, 52
Bell, Elliott V., x
Bell Telephone Laboratories, 61, 63, 71–76, 79, 81, 85–88, 95–97
Bell Telephone System, 70, 75
Bendix Corporation, 177
Berlin, 182, 187
Bhilai, 197, 198
Booms, speculative, 133, 134
Brain power, increasing supply of, 113–117
  in labor force, 108–111
  shortage of, 106–108

Brain power, shortage of, in transistor industry, 96–98
Brattain, Walter H., 71, 72
Brozen, Yale, 216, 232
Brush Beryllium Co., 177
Bureau of Labor Statistics, 33–36, 218, 219
Business cycles, 133–135
Business and Labor Advisory Research Councils, 34
Business Week, 135

Cairo, 198
Calculating devices, research on, 165
California Institute of Technology, 115
Capitalism as creator of science, 121–123
Carborundum Corporation, 118
Census Bureau, 218
Central Intelligence Agency, 194
Chaplin, Charlie, 103
China, Communist, 150, 183, 185–187, 191
Circuits, solid-state, 67
Cobbs, John L., x
Colborn, Robert B., x
Colleges and universities, 113–117, 232
  research and development in, tables, 234–237
Committee for Economic Development, 25, 135, 149, 196, 201
Communications, research in, 165–166
Communism, threat of, 13, 181–191
  (*See also* Soviet Union)
Computers, transistors in, 64
Conformity, 99–102
Copyrights, 4–5
Corning Glass Works, 177
Corporations and individual freedom, 123–125